Clash & Create
"Harnessing the Power of Opposition to Drive Innovation and Growth"

Kevin Griffiths

Clash & Create

Copyright © 2024 Kevin Griffiths

All rights reserved.

ISBN: 9798301534393

CONTENTS

1. Introduction: The Dialectical Journey Begins
2. Foundations of Dialectical Thinking
3. Embracing Opposition for Innovation
4. Strategic Synthesis: Crafting Winning Strategies
5. Cultivating a Culture of Innovation and Openness
6. Decision-Making Reimagined
7. Transforming Conflicts into Collaborative Success
8. Thriving in Change: The Dialectical Business
9. Implementing Dialectical Thinking in Your Business
10. The Dialectical Leader: Leading from the Front
11. Beyond Business: Dialectics in Personal Growth and Society
12. Harnessing Technology for Dialectical Innovation
13. Case Studies of Failure: When Dialectical Thinking Was Missing
14. Case Studies of Success: Thriving Through Synthesis
15. The Future of Dialectical Thinking
16. Cultural Impacts on Dialectical Thinking
17. Reflections and the Future of Dialectical Thinking

Introduction: The Dialectical Journey Begins

The Importance of Dialectics in Modern Business

In today's fast-changing and interconnected world, businesses face unprecedented levels of complexity. The rise of disruptive technologies, global markets, and shifting consumer behaviors has created an environment where traditional, linear approaches to problem-solving are no longer sufficient. To thrive in this landscape, organizations need a new mindset—one that embraces complexity, fosters creativity, and leverages the tension of opposing ideas. This is where dialectical thinking comes in.

Dialectics, a methodology rooted in the synthesis of opposites, provides a framework for navigating and resolving conflict. At its core, it involves identifying a starting position (**thesis**), understanding its contradiction or opposition (**antithesis**), and combining the two to create a more evolved solution (**synthesis**). Far from being a purely theoretical construct, this approach is deeply practical. It enables businesses to transform challenges into opportunities and to view conflict not as a barrier but as a powerful catalyst for innovation.

Consider the rapid pace of change in industries such as technology, healthcare, and retail. Companies that succeed are those that recognize the need for constant adaptation. They acknowledge competing priorities and perspectives—be it balancing short-term profits with long-term sustainability or integrating traditional practices with disruptive innovations—and use them to build stronger, more resilient strategies.

The ability to turn these opposing forces into drivers of progress is the hallmark of dialectical thinking. In today's business world, this approach is not just an advantage; it is essential for survival.

Overview of the Book's Structure and How to Use It

"Clash & Create" is a comprehensive guide to the principles and applications of dialectical thinking in business. It equips leaders, teams, and organizations with the tools to address complex challenges, drive innovation, and adapt to change. The book is structured to build a thorough understanding of dialectical principles while providing practical, actionable strategies for applying them.

Part One: Foundations and Principles

The first section explores the historical origins and evolution of dialectical thinking. It introduces foundational concepts—thesis, antithesis, and synthesis—and examines how these principles can be applied to complex decision-making, conflict resolution, and strategic planning.

Part Two: Dialectics in Action

This section focuses on practical applications. From fostering a culture of innovation to transforming conflicts into opportunities, each chapter offers case studies, techniques, and exercises to help readers embed dialectical thinking into their organizations.

Part Three: Leadership and Beyond

The final section examines the qualities of a dialectical leader and explores how organizations can cultivate a culture of openness and collaboration. It also extends the discussion beyond business, showing how dialectical thinking can contribute to personal growth and societal progress.

How to Use This Book

While the chapters build on each other to form a cohesive framework, they are also designed to be self-contained. Readers can explore the sections most relevant to their immediate challenges and return to other chapters as needed. Throughout the book, you will find reflective questions, exercises, and tools to deepen your understanding and facilitate application.

The Promise of Dialectical Thinking

By adopting a dialectical approach, businesses can navigate complexity with agility and insight. This mindset transforms problems into possibilities, conflicts into collaboration, and stagnation into innovation. The principles of dialectical thinking empower organizations to thrive in uncertainty, build stronger relationships, and achieve sustainable success.

As you embark on this journey, this book will guide you through the art and science of dialectics, equipping you with the skills to synthesize diverse perspectives and embrace the power of change. Welcome to a world where every clash becomes a chance to create something greater.

Chapter 1: Foundations of Dialectical Thinking

The Historical Roots of Dialectical Thinking

Dialectical thinking, though often associated with modern problem-solving and innovation, has its roots in ancient philosophy. Its evolution spans centuries and civilizations, influencing not only academic thought but also practical disciplines like governance, science, and now, business.

Socrates and the Birth of Dialectics

The seeds of dialectical thinking were sown in ancient Greece, where Socrates, one of history's most celebrated philosophers, introduced the concept of dialectic through his method of questioning. Known today as the **Socratic Method**, this approach involved probing questions that challenged assumptions, clarified concepts, and sought deeper understanding. For Socrates, truth emerged not from unilateral assertions but from dialogue, debate, and the critical examination of opposing ideas.

This method emphasized two fundamental principles:

1. **Critical Reflection:** By questioning the validity of existing beliefs, individuals could identify contradictions and refine their understanding.

2. **Collaborative Discovery:** Through dialogue, individuals could collectively arrive at more profound insights than they could alone.

Plato's Forms and Dialectical Idealism

Socrates' pupil, Plato, expanded on these ideas, elevating dialectical thinking to the realm of metaphysics. For Plato, dialectics was a journey from the tangible to the intangible, from the imperfect material world to the ideal realm of forms. His dialogues showcased dialectical processes as a means of ascending toward higher truths, blending logic with exploration.

Hegel's Triadic Structure

Fast forward to the 19th century, and dialectics took a new form under the German philosopher **Georg Wilhelm Friedrich Hegel**. Hegelian dialectics introduced a systematic structure:

- **Thesis:** An existing idea or state of affairs.
- **Antithesis:** A contradiction or challenge to the thesis.

- **Synthesis:** A reconciliation that integrates elements of both thesis and antithesis, resulting in a new and more advanced state.

Hegel's triadic model demonstrated that progress—whether in ideas, societies, or systems—arises from the dynamic interplay of opposing forces. This cyclical process ensures constant evolution and refinement.

Modern Adaptations

In the 20th century, dialectical thinking influenced diverse fields, from Karl Marx's critique of capitalism to advancements in scientific methodologies and educational practices. Today, its relevance extends into leadership, innovation, and organizational development, providing a timeless framework for navigating complexity and fostering growth.

Core Principles of Dialectics

Dialectical thinking revolves around three foundational principles that make it uniquely suited to addressing modern challenges.

1. Thesis, Antithesis, and Synthesis

At the heart of dialectics lies the interplay between thesis, antithesis, and synthesis:

- **Thesis:** The starting position or idea.
- **Antithesis:** A counterargument or opposing force.
- **Synthesis:** The integration of these opposing elements into a novel, higher-order solution.

This principle encourages critical examination of assumptions, open-mindedness toward opposing views, and creativity in resolving conflicts.

2. Conflict as a Catalyst for Growth

Rather than avoiding conflict, dialectics views it as a necessary condition for progress. When ideas clash, the resulting friction can illuminate hidden assumptions, reveal new perspectives, and inspire breakthroughs.

3. Continuous Evolution

Dialectical processes are iterative. Each synthesis becomes the new thesis, setting the stage for further antitheses and syntheses. This cycle fosters continuous learning, adaptation, and improvement, making it invaluable for dynamic and uncertain environments.

Real-World Applications of Dialectical Thinking

The principles of dialectical thinking are not confined to philosophical debates—they are actively shaping industries, organizations, and individual success stories. Below are some examples of how dialectical thinking manifests in real-world business contexts.

Product Innovation

A company's current product (thesis) may meet some customer needs but fail to address others. Customer feedback and competitor offerings (antithesis) highlight these gaps. By synthesizing these inputs, the company creates an enhanced product that outperforms its predecessor.

Example: Apple's evolution of the iPhone. With each iteration, customer complaints (antithesis) inform design improvements (synthesis), resulting in industry-leading products.

Leadership and Decision-Making

In leadership, dialectical thinking allows for balanced decisions that integrate diverse perspectives. A leader faced with conflicting departmental priorities (antitheses) can synthesize these viewpoints into a strategy that aligns with the organization's overarching goals.

Example: Starbucks' leadership during the 2008 financial crisis. The company balanced cost-cutting measures (thesis) with investment in employee benefits and training (antithesis), resulting in a revitalized brand (synthesis).

Conflict Resolution

In team settings, conflict often arises from differing opinions. A dialectical approach transforms these disagreements into opportunities for collaboration. By actively listening to all parties, identifying shared values, and combining ideas, teams can achieve outcomes that surpass initial expectations.

Example: Pixar Animation Studios' "Braintrust" sessions. These candid feedback meetings embrace conflict to improve creative works, often resulting in blockbuster films.

The Timeless Relevance of Dialectics

Dialectical thinking is not just a philosophical concept—it is a practical tool for navigating the complexities of modern life and business. By embracing its principles, organizations can foster innovation, resolve conflicts, and adapt to ever-changing environments. In the chapters ahead, we will explore how to apply these timeless ideas to specific business challenges, unlocking their full potential.

Chapter 2: Embracing Opposition for Innovation

The Value of Conflict in Driving Innovation

Innovation often springs from tension—the friction between what exists and what could be. Historically, some of the greatest breakthroughs emerged from conflicts between ideas, perspectives, or goals. Far from being a source of paralysis, opposition can act as a powerful catalyst for progress when harnessed effectively.

In the business world, opposition arises in many forms:

- Divergent viewpoints among team members.
- Competing priorities between departments.
- Customer demands versus operational constraints.

Rather than treating these conflicts as obstacles, organizations that embrace them discover opportunities for creativity, problem-solving, and transformation.

Why Conflict Fuels Innovation

- **Challenges Assumptions:** Opposition forces organizations to question the status quo, unearthing hidden assumptions that may no longer serve them.

- **Broadens Perspectives:** Differing opinions bring fresh ideas and alternative approaches to the table.

- **Drives Creative Solutions:** The effort to reconcile opposing views often leads to novel, higher-order solutions that would not have been possible in a uniform environment.

Example: The development of hybrid vehicles emerged from the tension between traditional internal combustion engines (thesis) and the environmental and efficiency demands of electric motors (antithesis). The synthesis—hybrid technology—has revolutionized the automotive industry.

Creating an Environment that Embraces Opposition

To unlock the potential of opposing ideas, organizations

must foster a culture where conflict is not only tolerated but actively encouraged. Achieving this requires deliberate strategies and leadership commitment.

1. Encourage Open Dialogue

Open dialogue ensures that diverse perspectives are voiced and heard. Teams must feel safe expressing dissenting opinions without fear of judgment or reprisal.

- **Leadership Role:** Leaders should model vulnerability by admitting mistakes, asking for feedback, and demonstrating openness to critique.

- **Practical Steps:** Create platforms for dialogue, such as brainstorming sessions, feedback forums, or cross-functional workshops.

Example: At Google, the "20% Time" initiative allows employees to dedicate a portion of their workweek to passion projects, fostering a culture of creativity and innovation.

2. Value Cognitive Diversity

Cognitive diversity—the inclusion of people with different ways of thinking, problem-solving, and decision-making—is a key driver of innovation. Teams that bring varied perspectives to the table are more likely to uncover creative solutions.

- **Recruiting for Diversity:** Prioritize hiring individuals from different cultural, educational, and professional backgrounds.
- **Fostering Inclusion:** Ensure that all voices are valued and amplified, particularly those that may be overlooked in traditional settings.

Example: Procter & Gamble's development of Swiffer products was driven by interdisciplinary teams that included engineers, marketers, and ethnographers. This diversity of thought led to an entirely new product category.

3. Reframe Conflict as Opportunity

Organizations must shift their mindset from seeing conflict as a source of dysfunction to recognizing it as a driver of progress. This reframing begins with language and practices.

- **Constructive Language:** Replace words like "argument" and "problem" with "discussion" and "challenge."
- **Facilitated Discussions:** Use skilled moderators to ensure that opposing viewpoints are explored constructively rather than devolving into personal attacks.

Example: Amazon's leadership principles emphasize "disagree and commit," encouraging employees to voice dissenting opinions while maintaining collective alignment once a decision is made.

Techniques for Harnessing Opposing Ideas

While creating an environment conducive to opposition is essential, it is equally important to have actionable techniques for turning that opposition into innovation.

1. Structured Debate

Encourage formalized debates where team members are assigned roles to argue for or against a particular idea. This forces individuals to think critically about both sides of an issue and often leads to unexpected insights.

- **Implementation:** Divide teams into proponents and skeptics of a strategy, with a neutral moderator to guide the discussion.

Example: IBM uses "Red Team/Blue Team" exercises to stress-test strategies, with one team identifying flaws and the other defending the plan.

2. Scenario Planning

Develop multiple future scenarios based on conflicting assumptions or priorities. This approach allows organizations to prepare for a range of possibilities and identify commonalities between divergent paths.

- **Steps:** Identify key variables (e.g., market trends, technological shifts), map out best-case and worst-case scenarios, and brainstorm solutions that address all contingencies.

Example: Shell Oil pioneered scenario planning in the 1970s, enabling the company to adapt successfully to volatile oil markets.

3. Design Thinking Workshops

Design thinking emphasizes empathy, experimentation, and iteration—perfect for reconciling opposition. Workshops bring diverse stakeholders together to co-create solutions by focusing on user needs.

- **Framework:**
- Define the problem (thesis).
- Gather insights from stakeholders (antithesis).
- Prototype and test solutions (synthesis).

Example: IDEO's design thinking approach has been instrumental in creating human-centered products, from healthcare innovations to consumer goods.

Case Studies: Innovation Born from Opposition

Pixar Animation Studios

Pixar's success is rooted in its ability to embrace creative conflict. In the company's "Braintrust" meetings, directors and creatives present works-in-progress and receive candid feedback from their peers. This often leads to heated debates but ultimately results in stronger, more refined films.

Takeaway: Creative conflict, when managed constructively, can elevate the quality of work far beyond initial expectations.

Airbnb

In its early days, Airbnb faced fierce opposition from regulators and traditional hotel lobbies. Rather than retreating, the company used this tension as an opportunity to innovate, working collaboratively with cities to develop regulations that benefited both parties.

Takeaway: Opposition from external stakeholders can drive innovation and create new industry norms.

Tesla's Electric Vehicles

Tesla's rise as an industry leader was fueled by its willingness to challenge the traditional automotive industry (thesis) with electric vehicles (antithesis). By integrating high-performance engineering with sustainability, Tesla synthesized a new model for transportation.

Takeaway: Challenging established norms often leads to revolutionary solutions.

Overcoming Barriers to Embracing Opposition

While the benefits of embracing opposition are clear, organizations often encounter barriers such as resistance to change, fear of conflict, or hierarchical silos. Addressing these challenges requires intentional strategies:

- **Training and Development:** Equip employees with skills in conflict resolution and active listening.

- **Leadership Commitment:** Ensure leaders champion open dialogue and model constructive behavior.

- **Feedback Loops:** Create mechanisms for continuous feedback to identify and address resistance early.

Conclusion

Opposition is not the enemy of progress—it is its engine. By fostering a culture that values conflict and implementing techniques to harness it effectively, organizations can unlock new levels of creativity and innovation. As we delve further into this journey, the next chapter will explore how these principles can be applied to strategic synthesis, crafting winning strategies that balance competing demands.

Chapter 3: Strategic Synthesis: Crafting Winning Strategies

The Art of Strategic Synthesis

In the dynamic landscape of modern business, strategy is rarely a straightforward roadmap. It is a delicate balancing act of competing priorities, diverse stakeholder needs, and rapidly changing market conditions. This complexity requires more than just traditional planning—it demands strategic synthesis.

Strategic synthesis is the process of merging divergent ideas, conflicting data, and opposing viewpoints into a cohesive, innovative strategy. It is a deliberate, iterative approach that allows businesses to integrate strengths and overcome contradictions, resulting in solutions that are both creative and actionable.

The Three Pillars of Strategic Synthesis

- **Thorough Analysis:** Understanding the thesis and antithesis of a situation by identifying key forces at play.

- **Collaborative Dialogue:** Engaging stakeholders to explore diverse perspectives and uncover hidden opportunities.

- **Visionary Integration:** Crafting a synthesis that aligns with organizational goals while addressing challenges and leveraging opportunities.

The Process of Synthesis in Business Strategy Development

Step 1: Define the Thesis and Antithesis

The first step in strategic synthesis is to clearly articulate the thesis (the current strategy, plan, or condition) and the antithesis (the opposing challenges, constraints, or alternative perspectives).

- **Example:** A retailer may define its thesis as focusing on physical store sales. The antithesis could be the rising consumer demand for e-commerce.

Step 2: Analyze Underlying Assumptions

Once the thesis and antithesis are defined, delve deeper into their underlying assumptions. This step reveals the factors driving both sides of the equation and identifies areas of misalignment or opportunity.

> **Example:** For the retailer, assumptions might include:

- Physical stores offer better customer experiences (thesis assumption).
- Consumers prioritize convenience over experience (antithesis assumption).

Step 3: Engage Stakeholders

Involve key stakeholders across departments, levels, and backgrounds. This step ensures that diverse perspectives are considered, reducing blind spots and increasing buy-in for the resulting strategy.

> **Example:** The retailer could include store managers, e-commerce specialists, and customer representatives in strategic discussions.

Step 4: Brainstorm and Develop the Synthesis

Bring together the insights from the thesis and antithesis to craft a synthesis—a new strategy that reconciles conflicts and leverages opportunities. This stage often requires creative thinking and iterative refinement.

> **Example:** The retailer's synthesis could involve creating an omnichannel strategy, blending physical store experiences with seamless e-commerce integration.

Step 5: Implement and Iterate

Deploy the synthesized strategy with clear action plans, measurable objectives, and ongoing feedback loops. Iteration ensures the strategy remains adaptable to new information or changing conditions.

> **Example:** The retailer could pilot an omnichannel approach in select markets, analyze performance metrics, and refine the model before scaling.

Tools and Frameworks for Strategic Synthesis

Strategic synthesis benefits from structured tools and frameworks that guide the process. Below are some of the most effective methods:

1. SWOT Analysis

A classic tool, SWOT (Strengths, Weaknesses, Opportunities, Threats) helps identify internal and external factors driving the thesis and antithesis.

> **Application:** Map strengths and weaknesses of the current strategy (thesis) against opportunities and threats posed by the environment (antithesis).

2. Scenario Planning

Scenario planning involves envisioning multiple future scenarios to explore the range of potential outcomes and strategies.

Steps:

- Identify key variables (e.g., market trends, regulatory changes).

- Develop plausible scenarios for each variable.

- Craft strategies that work across multiple scenarios.

  Example: Shell's scenario planning helped the company adapt to oil market volatility in the 1970s by preparing for both high-demand and low-demand scenarios.

3. Systems Thinking

Systems thinking views an organization as an interconnected network of parts, helping identify how changes in one area affect the whole.

> **Application:** Use systems mapping to visualize the interactions between competing strategies and identify leverage points for synthesis.

4. Balanced Scorecard

The balanced scorecard aligns business activities to organizational vision by balancing financial, customer, internal process, and learning/growth perspectives.

> **Application:** Evaluate strategies through multiple lenses to ensure the synthesis addresses holistic business objectives.

Case Studies: Strategic Synthesis in Action

1. Samsung Electronics: From Budget to Premium

In the early 2000s, Samsung faced a conflict between its reputation as a budget electronics manufacturer (thesis) and its ambition to compete with premium brands like Apple (antithesis). By synthesizing these positions, Samsung invested in high-end design and innovation while leveraging its cost-efficient manufacturing.

> **Outcome:** Samsung's Galaxy series emerged as a global leader, bridging affordability and premium quality.

2. Netflix: Adapting to the Streaming Revolution

Netflix began as a DVD rental service (thesis) but faced growing competition from digital streaming platforms (antithesis). Recognizing the shift in consumer behavior, Netflix synthesized its core strengths with streaming technology to become a global leader in digital entertainment.

> **Outcome:** Today, Netflix is a pioneer in both streaming and original content creation.

3. Patagonia: Profits with Purpose

Patagonia's commitment to environmental sustainability (thesis) initially clashed with traditional profit-driven business models (antithesis). By synthesizing these priorities, Patagonia implemented practices like using recycled materials and donating a portion of profits to environmental causes.

Outcome: The company built a loyal customer base while setting new standards for ethical business practices.

Overcoming Challenges in Strategic Synthesis

While strategic synthesis is a powerful approach, it is not without its challenges. Common obstacles include:

- **Resistance to Change:** Stakeholders may cling to the thesis, fearing disruption or uncertainty.

- **Polarization:** Strong opinions may prevent open dialogue, leading to deadlock.

- **Implementation Gaps:** A well-crafted synthesis can fail without clear execution plans.

Strategies for Overcoming Challenges

- **Facilitated Dialogue:** Use skilled moderators to guide discussions and mediate conflicts.

- **Prototyping:** Pilot synthesized strategies in small-scale implementations to build confidence and demonstrate value.

- **Clear Metrics:** Define measurable goals to track the success of the synthesis and refine as needed.

Conclusion

Strategic synthesis is both an art and a science. It allows organizations to navigate complexity by integrating opposing forces into unified, forward-looking strategies. Whether balancing tradition with innovation, short-term demands with long-term goals, or internal priorities with external pressures, the power of synthesis lies in its ability to create strategies that are not only robust but transformative.

The next chapter will explore how organizations can cultivate a culture that embraces dialectical thinking, fostering environments where innovation and collaboration thrive.

Chapter 4: Cultivating a Culture of Innovation and Openness

The Role of Culture in Driving Innovation

An organization's culture is its operating system, shaping how employees think, interact, and execute strategies. In environments where innovation is paramount, culture determines whether opposing ideas spark transformative breakthroughs or fizzle into unproductive friction. A culture that prioritizes openness, collaboration, and experimentation provides fertile ground for innovation to flourish.

Key Features of an Innovative Culture

- **Diverse Perspectives:** Diverse teams bring together varying viewpoints that challenge conventional thinking and fuel creativity.

- **Psychological Safety:** Employees feel secure sharing ideas, even those that challenge established norms.

- **Transparent Communication:** Clear, open channels foster trust and alignment.

- **Experimentation:** The freedom to test and iterate leads to breakthroughs while normalizing learning from failure.

Organizations that embed these qualities into their culture consistently outperform their peers in terms of adaptability, growth, and employee engagement.

The Leadership Imperative

Leaders act as cultural architects. Their behaviors, decisions, and communication styles set the tone for the organization. In cultivating innovation, leaders must:

- **Model Curiosity:** Actively seek input from diverse perspectives, demonstrating openness to ideas beyond their own.

- **Encourage Risk-Taking:** Reward bold thinking and make it clear that failure is a step toward progress.

- **Foster Inclusivity:** Create an environment where every team member feels valued and heard.

Leadership Case Study: Microsoft under Satya Nadella

When Satya Nadella took over as CEO of Microsoft in 2014, the company was struggling with internal silos, a rigid hierarchical culture, and declining relevance in the tech world. Nadella's approach to leadership emphasized empathy, collaboration, and continuous learning:

- He shifted the focus from internal competition to shared success, encouraging teams to work together across departments.

- By adopting a "growth mindset" philosophy, Nadella helped employees view challenges as opportunities rather than obstacles.

- He prioritized investments in emerging technologies like cloud computing and artificial intelligence.

Outcome: Microsoft's cultural transformation not only revitalized employee morale but also positioned the company as a leader in cloud technology, nearly tripling its market value within a decade.

Strategies for Cultivating Innovation and Openness

1. Build Diverse Teams

Diversity in thought and experience enriches problem-solving. Teams composed of individuals with different cultural, educational, and professional backgrounds are more likely to approach challenges creatively.

Action Plan:

- Recruit talent from varied industries and demographics.

- Promote inclusion by ensuring diverse voices are represented in leadership roles.

- Conduct training on unconscious bias to create an equitable workplace.

Case Study: Johnson & Johnson

Johnson & Johnson attributes much of its success in healthcare innovation to its commitment to diversity. By forming interdisciplinary teams of scientists, marketers, and ethnographers, the company has developed groundbreaking products like the first single-dose HIV treatment.

Positive Outcome: The integration of diverse expertise has enabled Johnson & Johnson to address global healthcare challenges effectively, maintaining its position as an industry leader for over a century.

2. Foster Psychological Safety

Employees who feel safe expressing their ideas and concerns are more engaged and innovative. Psychological safety enables candid discussions that bring hidden risks and opportunities to light.

Action Plan:

- Train managers to handle feedback constructively and to welcome challenges.

- Establish ground rules for respectful dialogue in meetings.

- Publicly acknowledge and reward team members who share bold or unconventional ideas.

Case Study: Google's High-Performing Teams

Google conducted a multi-year study called "Project Aristotle" to identify what makes teams effective. The research revealed that psychological safety—the belief that it's safe to take risks and speak up—is the most critical factor in team performance. To foster this, Google implemented regular check-ins, anonymous feedback tools, and team-building exercises.

Positive Outcome: Teams with high psychological safety consistently outperformed others in terms of innovation, collaboration, and productivity, enabling Google to maintain its reputation as a global tech innovator.

3. Encourage Constructive Conflict

Healthy conflict pushes teams to refine their ideas and uncover solutions that wouldn't emerge in a purely harmonious environment. Managed correctly, disagreements spark innovation rather than discord.

Action Plan:

- Use structured debate formats to explore competing perspectives.
- Appoint neutral facilitators to mediate contentious discussions.
- Frame disagreements as opportunities to align on the best solutions.

Case Study: Pixar Animation Studios

Pixar's "Braintrust" sessions are legendary for fostering creative conflict. In these meetings, directors present their works-in-progress to a trusted group of peers who provide candid feedback. The open exchange often leads to passionate debates but ultimately strengthens the final product.

Positive Outcome: This culture of constructive critique has enabled Pixar to produce some of the most beloved animated films in history, including *Toy Story*, *Finding Nemo*, and *Inside Out*. Every film benefits from the collective wisdom of the Braintrust, resulting in stories that resonate universally.

4. Emphasize Experimentation

Organizations that view failure as an essential part of learning are more likely to discover game-changing innovations. Experimentation involves testing new ideas, analyzing results, and iterating based on insights.

Action Plan:

- Dedicate resources for R&D and innovation labs.

- Establish a framework for piloting ideas on a small scale before full implementation.

- Celebrate learnings from failed experiments to reduce fear of risk-taking.

Case Study: Amazon's "Day 1" Philosophy

Jeff Bezos famously advocates for a "Day 1" mindset, emphasizing experimentation and adaptability. Amazon's culture encourages employees to innovate fearlessly, even if it means accepting short-term losses. This approach has driven innovations like Amazon Web Services (AWS), Alexa, and Prime delivery.

Positive Outcome: Amazon's willingness to experiment has enabled it to dominate multiple industries, from e-commerce to cloud computing, becoming one of the most valuable companies in the world.

5. Promote Transparent Communication

Clear and open communication aligns teams and ensures that employees understand how their contributions fit into the larger mission. Transparency fosters trust and collaboration, critical ingredients for an innovative culture.

Action Plan:

- Hold regular all-hands meetings to share progress and challenges.

- Use collaboration tools like Slack or Microsoft Teams to enhance real-time communication.

- Offer employees access to key decision-making processes through open forums or Q&A sessions.

Case Study: Patagonia

Patagonia's commitment to transparency extends beyond its environmental mission. The company openly shares its supply chain practices, sustainability goals, and financial performance with employees and customers alike. This openness fosters a sense of collective responsibility and engagement among stakeholders.

Positive Outcome: Patagonia's culture has attracted a loyal customer base and top-tier talent, while its innovative practices have set benchmarks for sustainability in the apparel industry.

Overcoming Cultural Resistance

Transforming an organization's culture is rarely easy. Resistance to change often arises from entrenched mindsets, fear of failure, or uncertainty about new expectations.

Common Barriers

- **Fear of Change:** Employees may resist new practices out of concern for job security or disruption.

- **Hierarchical Silos:** Rigid organizational structures can stifle collaboration across departments.

- **Inconsistent Leadership Support:** Without visible commitment from leaders, cultural initiatives can falter.

- **Strategies to Overcome Resistance**

- **Communicate a Clear Vision:** Articulate the purpose and benefits of cultural change at every level of the organization.

- **Start with Small Wins:** Pilot new cultural practices in specific teams or projects to demonstrate success and build momentum.

- **Engage Change Champions:** Identify influential employees to advocate for innovation and openness within their networks.

Conclusion

An innovative culture doesn't emerge by chance—it is cultivated through deliberate actions, strong leadership, and sustained effort. By fostering diverse teams, encouraging psychological safety, and promoting transparent communication, organizations can unlock the full potential of their workforce. The next chapter will build on these principles by exploring how dialectical thinking transforms decision-making processes, enabling leaders to navigate complexity with clarity.

Clash & Create

Chapter 5: Decision-Making Reimagined

The Evolution of Decision-Making

In traditional business environments, decision-making often follows a linear process: gather data, analyze options, and choose the most logical course of action. While this method works in stable and predictable contexts, it struggles to address the complexity and ambiguity of modern business challenges. In a world of rapid change and competing priorities, decision-making requires a more dynamic and iterative approach.

Dialectical decision-making embraces complexity by acknowledging that multiple, often conflicting, perspectives are valuable. It transforms decision-making from a static process into a dynamic dialogue that seeks synthesis between opposing ideas.

Key Characteristics of Dialectical Decision-Making

1. **Inclusive:** It involves diverse stakeholders to ensure all relevant perspectives are considered.

2. **Adaptive:** It incorporates new information and adjusts strategies as circumstances evolve.

3. **Innovative:** It uses tension between opposing views to generate creative solutions.

Traditional vs. Dialectical Decision-Making

Traditional Decision-Making

- Follows a linear, top-down approach.
- Focuses on minimizing conflict and prioritizing efficiency.
- Assumes stability and predictability.

Dialectical Decision-Making

- Encourages exploration of conflicting ideas and perspectives.
- Leverages conflict as a source of insight and innovation.
- Embraces uncertainty and adapts to change dynamically.

The Dialectical Decision-Making Process

Step 1: Define the Decision Context

Clearly articulate the problem or opportunity at hand, including its scope, impact, and stakeholders involved. Understanding the context ensures the decision aligns with broader organizational goals.

> **Example:** A software company deciding whether to prioritize mobile app development (thesis) or desktop app improvements (antithesis).

Step 2: Gather Diverse Perspectives

Engage stakeholders with varying roles, experiences, and viewpoints to uncover the full spectrum of considerations. This step is critical for identifying both the thesis and antithesis of the decision.

> **Example:** The software company involves developers, marketers, and customer service teams to understand the technical challenges, market trends, and user feedback.

Step 3: Analyze Conflicts and Contradictions

Encourage open discussions to explore conflicts between the thesis and antithesis. Identify the assumptions, risks, and opportunities associated with each perspective.

> **Example:** Developers highlight technical limitations of mobile platforms, while marketers argue for the growing demand for mobile apps.

Step 4: Synthesize a Solution

Integrate the most compelling aspects of the thesis and antithesis into a cohesive solution. This synthesis should address the identified conflicts while leveraging opportunities.

> **Example:** The company develops a hybrid strategy, launching a scaled-down mobile app while enhancing desktop features to cater to both markets.

Step 5: Implement and Iterate

Deploy the decision with measurable goals and clear timelines. Monitor outcomes and remain open to revisiting the synthesis if new information emerges.

> **Example:** The software company tracks user adoption and feedback for the mobile app, using insights to refine future updates.

Tools for Dialectical Decision-Making

1. Fishbone Diagrams

Also known as cause-and-effect diagrams, these tools help visualize the root causes of a problem and explore potential solutions from multiple angles.

> **Use Case:** Analyze the factors contributing to declining customer retention and identify conflicting approaches to address them.

2. Decision Trees

Decision trees map out possible choices and their consequences, helping teams evaluate the trade-offs between competing options.

> **Use Case:** Compare the financial and operational impacts of expanding into new markets versus focusing on existing customers.

3. Delphi Method

This structured communication technique involves gathering input from a panel of experts through multiple rounds of questioning to reach a consensus.

> **Use Case:** Develop strategies for navigating regulatory changes in a heavily regulated industry like pharmaceuticals.

Case Studies: Dialectical Decision-Making in Action

Case Study 1: Patagonia's Environmental Commitment

Patagonia faced a decision between maintaining its profit margins (thesis) and doubling down on environmental sustainability (antithesis). By engaging stakeholders across the company, Patagonia synthesized a strategy that integrated sustainability into its core business model. Initiatives included using recycled materials, encouraging customers to repair products, and donating 1% of sales to environmental causes.

Positive Outcome: The approach not only reinforced Patagonia's brand identity but also attracted a loyal customer base, boosting long-term profitability.

Case Study 2: Best Buy's Omnichannel Strategy

In the early 2010s, Best Buy struggled with "showrooming," where customers browsed in-store but purchased online from competitors like Amazon. Initially, the company focused solely on improving in-store experiences (thesis), but this failed to address the growing trend of online shopping (antithesis). Best Buy synthesized these approaches by launching an omnichannel strategy that integrated online and in-store experiences. Initiatives included price-matching, same-day pickup, and in-store digital consultations.

Positive Outcome: Best Buy's ability to embrace both digital and physical retail resulted in a remarkable turnaround, increasing market share and profitability.

Case Study 3: NASA's Apollo 13 Mission

When an oxygen tank exploded during the Apollo 13 mission, NASA faced a life-or-death decision: abandon the mission (thesis) or attempt an unprecedented rescue (antithesis). Engineers and astronauts used a dialectical approach to brainstorm and synthesize creative solutions. By leveraging limited resources and thinking outside traditional protocols, they developed a plan to return the crew safely.

Positive Outcome: The successful rescue of the Apollo 13 crew became a defining moment in NASA's history, showcasing the power of collaborative and adaptive decision-making.

Overcoming Challenges in Dialectical Decision-Making

While dialectical decision-making offers significant advantages, it also presents challenges. Common obstacles include:

1. **Paralysis by Analysis:** Overanalyzing conflicts can delay decisions.

2. **Resistance to Change:** Stakeholders may resist synthesizing approaches that challenge traditional methods.

3. **Lack of Facilitation Skills:** Poorly managed discussions can lead to unproductive debates.

Strategies for Success

1. **Set Clear Timelines:** Establish deadlines for each stage of the process to avoid delays.

2. **Provide Facilitation Training:** Equip managers with skills to mediate conflicts and guide discussions constructively.

3. **Prioritize Experimentation:** Treat decisions as iterative processes rather than final verdicts, allowing room for adjustments.

Conclusion

Dialectical decision-making reimagines how organizations navigate complexity. By embracing opposing ideas and leveraging tension as a creative force, this approach drives smarter, more innovative decisions. From addressing environmental challenges to navigating market disruptions, the principles of synthesis empower businesses to achieve outcomes that are both practical and visionary.

The next chapter will focus on conflict transformation, exploring how dialectical methods can turn disagreements into collaborative successes.

Chapter 6: Transforming Conflicts into Collaborative Success

Understanding the Nature of Conflict in Business

Conflict is an inevitable part of any organization, arising from differences in goals, values, or perspectives. While often perceived as negative, conflict, when approached constructively, can become a powerful driver of collaboration, innovation, and progress.

Common Sources of Business Conflict

1. **Competing Priorities:** Departments or teams with differing objectives may clash over resource allocation or strategic focus.

2. **Cultural Differences:** Diverse teams bring varying approaches to work, decision-making, and communication.

3. **Miscommunication:** Ambiguities in messaging or lack of transparency can lead to misunderstandings and tension.

4. **Role Ambiguity:** Overlapping responsibilities or unclear boundaries can create friction among employees.

The Opportunity in Conflict

Rather than viewing conflict as a problem to avoid, successful organizations see it as an opportunity to:

- **Surface Hidden Issues:** Conflicts often highlight underlying challenges that need attention.

- **Generate Creative Solutions:** Tensions between opposing ideas can inspire innovative approaches.

- **Strengthen Relationships:** Constructively resolving conflicts builds trust and mutual respect.

The Dialectical Approach to Conflict Resolution

Dialectical methods transform conflicts into opportunities by synthesizing opposing perspectives. This approach emphasizes understanding, collaboration, and integration, fostering outcomes that benefit all parties.

Step 1: Identify Underlying Assumptions

Encourage all parties to articulate their positions and the assumptions underlying them. This process clarifies the root causes of the conflict.

> **Example:** In a clash between marketing and product development teams, the marketing team may assume rapid launches drive competitive advantage, while the product team prioritizes quality and reliability.

Step 2: Create a Safe Space for Dialogue

Establish a forum where all parties feel heard and respected. Use neutral facilitators or structured discussions to ensure productive communication.

> **Action Plan:** Introduce a "no interruptions" rule, allowing each party to present their case fully before responding.

Step 3: Explore the Thesis and Antithesis

Encourage participants to articulate their thesis (their current stance) and antithesis (their concerns about the opposing view). This step reveals the values and priorities driving each position.

> **Example:** The marketing team's thesis might focus on competitive positioning, while their antithesis may involve fears of reputational damage from subpar products.

Step 4: Brainstorm Collaborative Solutions

Facilitate brainstorming sessions to identify a synthesis—solutions that integrate elements of both perspectives. Encourage participants to focus on shared goals rather than individual victories.

> **Example:** The teams agree to adopt a phased product launch strategy that balances rapid deployment with iterative quality improvements.

Step 5: Develop and Implement Actionable Plans

Translate the synthesis into concrete actions with clear responsibilities, timelines, and accountability measures. Regular check-ins ensure alignment and progress.

Techniques for Effective Conflict Resolution

1. Empathetic Listening

Empathy is the cornerstone of constructive conflict resolution. Listening to understand, rather than to rebut, fosters mutual respect and deeper insights.

> **Practical Tip:** Use paraphrasing techniques to confirm understanding, e.g., "What I hear you saying is..."

2. Socratic Questioning

Encourage critical thinking by asking open-ended questions that challenge assumptions and deepen understanding.

> **Example Questions:**
>
> - "What outcomes are most important to you?"
> - "How might this approach address your concerns?"

3. Collaborative Negotiation

Focus on interests rather than positions. By identifying shared objectives, parties can co-create solutions that satisfy underlying needs.

> **Framework:** Use the "interest-based bargaining" approach:
>
> 1. Identify shared goals.
>
> 2. Explore multiple options.
>
> 3. Evaluate solutions based on mutual benefit.

4. Conflict Mapping

Visualize the conflict by mapping out stakeholders, their positions, and the relationships between them. This tool highlights areas of alignment and tension.

> **Use Case:** A team experiencing tension between senior management and junior staff can use mapping to pinpoint gaps in expectations and communication.

Case Studies: Collaborative Conflict Resolution

Case Study 1: LEGO's Organizational Turnaround

In the early 2000s, LEGO faced financial struggles exacerbated by internal conflicts. Marketing wanted to pursue trend-driven products, while designers advocated for traditional, timeless toys. The tension between these priorities created paralysis and poor product alignment.

Resolution: LEGO adopted a dialectical approach, synthesizing both perspectives. They developed innovative products like LEGO Mindstorms, which combined modern technology with classic building experiences. Cross-departmental collaboration became a central tenet of their strategy.

Positive Outcome: LEGO's turnaround was dramatic, transforming it into one of the most profitable and beloved toy companies in the world.

Case Study 2: Southwest Airlines and Labor Relations

The airline industry is notorious for contentious labor relations, but Southwest Airlines stands out for its collaborative approach. When disagreements arise, the company prioritizes dialogue and mutual respect.

Resolution: Southwest engages unions and employees in decision-making processes, ensuring transparency and shared accountability. Their culture emphasizes problem-solving through partnership rather than adversarial tactics.

Positive Outcome: Southwest consistently ranks high in employee satisfaction and operational efficiency, demonstrating that collaboration can lead to enduring success.

Case Study 3: Ben & Jerry's Social Mission Alignment

Ben & Jerry's faced internal conflicts between its social

mission and corporate profitability. Some stakeholders pushed for cost-cutting measures, while others prioritized ethical sourcing and sustainability.

Resolution: By engaging employees, customers, and suppliers in structured dialogues, Ben & Jerry's identified a synthesis: they would invest in sustainable practices while leveraging their social mission as a unique selling point.

Positive Outcome: The company grew its market share while maintaining its ethical commitments, proving that profitability and purpose can coexist.

Overcoming Challenges in Transforming Conflict

Even with the best intentions, transforming conflict into collaboration is not always straightforward. Common challenges include:

1. **Entrenched Positions:** Participants may resist compromise, fearing loss of influence or credibility.

2. **Emotional Reactions:** Strong emotions can escalate conflicts, hindering rational discussion.

3. **Lack of Facilitation Skills:** Poorly managed conflicts may deepen divisions rather than resolve them.

Strategies for Overcoming Challenges

1. **Neutral Facilitation:** Use skilled mediators to guide discussions and defuse tension.

2. **Focus on Shared Goals:** Reframe the conflict as a joint problem to solve rather than a competition to win.

3. **Provide Training:** Equip employees with conflict resolution skills through workshops and role-playing exercises.

Conclusion

Conflict, when managed constructively, is not a liability but a powerful tool for innovation and collaboration. By adopting dialectical methods, organizations can transform disagreements into opportunities for growth, aligning diverse perspectives toward shared success. The next chapter will explore how these principles of collaboration and synthesis can help organizations thrive in a constantly changing world.

Chapter 7: Thriving in Change: The Dialectical Business

The Importance of Adaptability in Modern Business

In today's volatile business environment, change is not an exception—it is the rule. Rapid technological advancements, shifting consumer preferences, and global disruptions demand that organizations evolve continuously. Businesses that cling to traditional methods risk irrelevance, while those that embrace adaptability thrive.

Why Adaptability Matters

1. **Resilience:** Organizations that anticipate and adapt to change can weather disruptions and emerge stronger.

2. **Opportunity Recognition:** Adaptable businesses identify and capitalize on emerging trends before competitors.

3. **Customer Alignment:** Continuous adaptation ensures that products and services remain relevant to evolving customer needs.

Challenges to Adaptability

- **Resistance to Change:** Employees and leaders may resist new approaches due to fear of failure or comfort with the status quo.

- **Complexity:** Rapid change often brings ambiguity, making it difficult to predict outcomes.

- **Resource Constraints:** Adapting to change requires investments in time, talent, and technology.

Dialectical Thinking as a Framework for Change

Dialectical thinking equips organizations to navigate change by synthesizing stability and innovation. It recognizes that successful adaptation involves balancing competing priorities, such as:

- Preserving core values while embracing new strategies.

- Managing short-term disruptions while planning for long-term growth.

- Addressing internal resistance while fostering enthusiasm for change.

The Dialectical Approach to Change

1. **Identify the Thesis:** Define the current state, including established processes, strengths, and limitations.

2. **Explore the Antithesis:** Examine the drivers of change, such as market shifts, technological advancements, or customer feedback.

3. **Develop the Synthesis:** Create a strategy that integrates the strengths of the thesis with the demands of the antithesis.

Steps to Build an Adaptable, Dialectical Organization

1. Cultivate a Growth Mindset

A growth mindset encourages employees and leaders to view challenges as opportunities for learning and development.

Action Plan:
- Recognize and reward employees who embrace new approaches.
- Provide training to build skills and confidence in navigating change.

- Share success stories that highlight the benefits of adaptability.

Example: Microsoft's cultural shift under Satya Nadella emphasized a growth mindset, enabling the company to pivot toward cloud computing and artificial intelligence successfully.

2. Build Agile Systems

Agile systems allow organizations to respond quickly to changing circumstances by prioritizing flexibility and experimentation.

Action Plan:
- Implement agile project management frameworks like Scrum or Kanban.
- Encourage iterative processes, where solutions are developed, tested, and refined in cycles.
- Reduce bureaucratic hurdles that slow decision-making.

Example: Spotify's "Squad" system fosters agility by empowering cross-functional teams to develop, test, and iterate on features independently, keeping the company at the forefront of music streaming innovation.

3. Balance Tradition and Innovation

While innovation is essential for adaptation, organizations must also preserve the aspects of their identity that resonate with stakeholders.

Action Plan:

- Define core values that anchor the organization during change.

- Evaluate which processes or practices support innovation, and which hinder it.

- Engage stakeholders to align on what aspects of the organization's legacy should be preserved.

Example: The New York Times transitioned successfully to digital media by synthesizing its commitment to journalistic excellence (tradition) with cutting-edge digital storytelling methods (innovation).

4. Foster Collaboration Across Silos

Cross-functional collaboration ensures that diverse perspectives are incorporated into change initiatives, reducing blind spots and increasing buy-in.

Action Plan:

- Break down silos by forming cross-departmental task forces.

- Use collaborative tools like Slack, Microsoft Teams, or Asana to enhance communication.

- Facilitate regular meetings where departments share insights and align strategies.

Example: Ford's shift to electric vehicles involved

collaboration across engineering, design, marketing, and sustainability teams, enabling the company to integrate environmental goals with consumer expectations.

Case Studies: Businesses Thriving Amidst Change

Case Study 1: Netflix's Evolution

Netflix began as a DVD rental service, but its leaders recognized the growing potential of streaming technology. By embracing change, Netflix transitioned to a streaming model while also becoming a leader in content creation.

Dialectical Approach:

- **Thesis:** Maintain customer-centric service through DVD rentals.

- **Antithesis:** Address the growing demand for instant, on-demand content.

- **Synthesis:** Transition to a streaming-first model and invest in original programming.

Positive Outcome: Netflix became a global entertainment powerhouse, disrupting traditional media and redefining the industry.

Case Study 2: Adobe's Move to Subscription Services

Adobe faced declining sales as customers hesitated to purchase expensive, one-time software licenses. Recognizing the shift toward cloud-based services, Adobe transitioned to a subscription model.

Dialectical Approach:

- **Thesis:** Preserve Adobe's reputation for high-quality creative tools.

- **Antithesis:** Address customer demand for affordability and flexibility.

- **Synthesis:** Develop Adobe Creative Cloud, offering subscription-based access to its entire suite.

Positive Outcome: The subscription model revitalized Adobe's business, increasing revenue consistency and expanding its user base.

Case Study 3: LEGO's Adaptation to Digital Play

LEGO, a company known for its physical building blocks, faced declining sales due to the rise of digital entertainment. Instead of resisting this trend, LEGO embraced it by integrating digital experiences with its traditional products.

Dialectical Approach:

- **Thesis:** Preserve the tactile, creative nature of LEGO play.

- **Antithesis:** Address the growing demand for digital interactivity.

- **Synthesis:** Launch hybrid products like LEGO Mindstorms and LEGO Super Mario, blending physical and digital elements.

Positive Outcome: LEGO maintained its iconic status while appealing to a new generation of tech-savvy consumers.

Overcoming Resistance to Change

Resistance to change is a natural reaction, but it can be mitigated through intentional strategies that build trust and engagement.

Common Barriers

1. **Fear of Failure:** Employees may worry about the risks associated with change.

2. **Loss of Control:** Leaders and teams may feel uneasy about shifting responsibilities or processes.

3. **Unclear Vision:** Ambiguity about the purpose or benefits of change can create skepticism.

Strategies to Address Resistance

1. **Communicate Clearly:** Share a compelling vision for change, including the "why" and "how."

2. **Involve Stakeholders:** Engage employees in decision-making processes to build ownership.

3. **Provide Support:** Offer training, resources, and mentorship to help employees navigate transitions.

Conclusion

Adaptability is the cornerstone of success in a constantly evolving business environment. By using dialectical thinking, organizations can balance tradition and innovation, fostering resilience and agility. Through a structured approach to change, businesses can not only survive disruptions but turn them into opportunities for growth and leadership. In the next chapter, we will explore practical steps for embedding dialectical thinking into your organization, transforming it into a dynamic and innovative powerhouse.

Clash & Create

Chapter 8: Implementing Dialectical Thinking in Your Business

The Practical Path to Embedding Dialectical Thinking

Dialectical thinking offers a transformative framework for organizations to navigate complexity, foster innovation, and adapt to change. However, integrating this mindset requires deliberate actions across cultural, structural, and procedural levels.

Key Benefits of Dialectical Thinking

1. **Enhanced Problem-Solving:** Encourages holistic perspectives and creative solutions.

2. **Stronger Collaboration:** Fosters mutual understanding and alignment among diverse stakeholders.

3. **Continuous Adaptation:** Positions organizations to evolve dynamically in response to new challenges.

Embedding dialectical thinking is not a one-time initiative but an ongoing journey that involves cultural shifts, capacity building, and sustained leadership commitment.

Step 1: Assess Current Organizational Culture

Before implementing dialectical thinking, organizations must evaluate their current culture to identify strengths, weaknesses, and areas for improvement.

Assessment Areas

- **Openness to Dissent:** Are employees encouraged to challenge the status quo?

- **Decision-Making Processes:** Do current practices incorporate diverse perspectives?

- **Adaptability:** How quickly does the organization respond to change?

Action Plan: Cultural Audit

1. Conduct surveys and focus groups to gather employee feedback on decision-making and openness to conflict.

2. Evaluate case studies of past successes and failures to identify patterns in organizational behavior.

3. Benchmark against industry peers to assess cultural competitiveness.

Step 2: Engage Leadership

Leadership is the driving force behind cultural transformation. Leaders must model dialectical thinking and champion its integration across the organization.

Qualities of Dialectical Leaders

- **Empathy:** Understand and value diverse viewpoints.

- **Critical Thinking:** Challenge assumptions and explore alternatives.

- **Vision:** Align dialectical practices with long-term organizational goals.

Action Plan: Leadership Development

1. Provide training on dialectical thinking, including workshops on conflict resolution, synthesis techniques, and collaborative decision-making.

2. Establish leadership forums where executives can practice and refine their dialectical approaches.

3. Hold leaders accountable for fostering open dialogue and inclusive practices within their teams.

Step 3: Build Skills Across the Organization

For dialectical thinking to thrive, employees at all levels must develop the skills and confidence to apply it in their daily work.

Training Focus Areas

1. **Conflict Resolution:** Teach employees how to navigate disagreements constructively.

2. **Socratic Questioning:** Encourage critical inquiry to uncover deeper insights.

3. **Creative Problem-Solving:** Equip teams with tools to generate innovative solutions.

Action Plan: Organization-Wide Training

- Develop customized training programs tailored to different roles and levels within the organization.

- Use experiential learning methods, such as role-playing and case studies, to reinforce concepts.

- Offer ongoing support through mentorship programs and peer learning groups.

Step 4: Introduce Dialectical Processes

Structural changes are necessary to sustain dialectical thinking. This involves embedding it into organizational processes, from strategic planning to daily operations.

Examples of Dialectical Processes

- **Decision-Making Frameworks:** Use structured methods, such as thesis-antithesis-synthesis, to guide strategic decisions.

- **Feedback Mechanisms:** Create systems for capturing diverse perspectives, such as suggestion boxes, regular surveys, or brainstorming sessions.

- **Project Planning:** Incorporate iterative reviews where opposing viewpoints are evaluated and synthesized.

Case Study: IBM's Decision-Making Process

IBM implemented "Design Thinking" workshops to integrate dialectical methods into its innovation processes. These sessions brought together cross-functional teams to explore challenges, articulate opposing perspectives, and co-create solutions.

Positive Outcome: IBM significantly accelerated its product development cycles, fostering customer-centric innovations that strengthened its competitive position.

Step 5: Foster Cross-Functional Collaboration

Collaboration across departments ensures that dialectical thinking is applied holistically, breaking down silos and integrating diverse expertise.

Action Plan: Collaboration Initiatives

1. Establish cross-departmental task forces to tackle strategic challenges.

2. Rotate employees across teams to foster interdisciplinary understanding.

3. Use collaboration tools like Slack, Trello, or Miro to facilitate real-time communication and idea sharing.

Case Study: Unilever's Sustainability Strategy

Unilever formed cross-functional teams to align its sustainability goals with its business strategy. By synthesizing input from marketing, R&D, and supply chain teams, the company launched eco-friendly products without compromising profitability.

Positive Outcome: Unilever gained a competitive edge while advancing its commitment to environmental and social responsibility.

Step 6: Measure and Refine

Continuous improvement is essential for embedding dialectical thinking. Organizations must establish metrics to evaluate progress and identify areas for refinement.

Key Metrics

- **Innovation Outputs:** Number and quality of new products, services, or processes.

- **Employee Engagement:** Levels of participation in decision-making and collaboration initiatives.

- **Adaptation Speed:** Time taken to respond to market changes or disruptions.

Action Plan: Feedback Loops

1. Conduct regular reviews of dialectical initiatives to assess their impact.

2. Use surveys and focus groups to gather feedback from employees and stakeholders.

3. Refine training, processes, and structures based on insights from these evaluations.

Case Study: Netflix's Iterative Approach

Netflix uses continuous feedback loops to evaluate the success of its content and user interface. By integrating customer feedback with internal data, the company iteratively refines its offerings to stay ahead in the competitive streaming market.

Positive Outcome: Netflix's adaptive processes have enabled it to retain its market leadership and expand its global reach.

Common Challenges and How to Overcome Them

Challenge 1: Resistance to Change

Employees may resist dialectical initiatives due to fear of the unknown or skepticism about their effectiveness.

> **Solution:** Communicate the purpose and benefits of dialectical thinking through clear, consistent messaging. Share success stories to build trust and enthusiasm.

Challenge 2: Lack of Alignment

Departments may struggle to align on goals or processes, undermining dialectical efforts.

> **Solution:** Use facilitated sessions to identify shared objectives and build consensus around synthesis-driven strategies.

Challenge 3: Skill Gaps

Not all employees may feel equipped to engage in dialectical processes.

> **Solution:** Offer tailored training and resources to build confidence and capabilities across the workforce.

Conclusion

Implementing dialectical thinking transforms organizations into dynamic, innovative, and adaptable systems. By fostering a culture of openness, equipping employees with the right skills, and embedding dialectical methods into everyday processes, businesses can navigate complexity with confidence and clarity.

The next chapter will explore the qualities of a dialectical leader, examining how individuals can lead by example and inspire their teams to embrace synthesis and collaboration.

Chapter 9: The Dialectical Leader: Leading from the Front

The Role of Leadership in a Dialectical Organization

Leadership is the cornerstone of a dialectical organization. Dialectical leaders guide teams through the complexity of modern business by synthesizing opposing ideas, fostering collaboration, and modeling adaptability. They create environments where innovation thrives, conflicts are constructive, and employees feel empowered to contribute their best work.

Why Dialectical Leadership Matters

1. **Navigating Complexity:** Leaders must manage competing priorities, such as balancing short-term results with long-term goals.

2. **Fostering Collaboration:** Dialectical leaders break down silos and encourage diverse perspectives, creating synergy across teams.

3. **Inspiring Adaptability:** By embracing change and uncertainty, they set the tone for resilience and continuous improvement.

Key Characteristics of a Dialectical Leader

1. Open-Mindedness

Dialectical leaders value diverse viewpoints and remain receptive to new ideas, even when they challenge their own beliefs.

> **Example:** Indra Nooyi, former CEO of PepsiCo, regularly sought input from employees at all levels, using their insights to inform her bold strategies for sustainability and innovation.

2. Emotional Intelligence

Understanding and managing emotions—both their own and those of others—enables leaders to navigate conflicts and build trust.

> **Example:** Satya Nadella's empathetic leadership transformed Microsoft's culture, fostering a sense of psychological safety and collaboration.

3. Visionary Thinking

Dialectical leaders balance immediate challenges with long-term aspirations, crafting strategies that inspire teams while addressing practical realities.

> **Example:** Elon Musk's vision for Tesla blends sustainability (long-term impact) with cutting-edge innovation (short-term differentiation).

4. Critical Thinking

They approach decisions analytically, questioning assumptions and seeking evidence to support their conclusions.

> **Example:** Amazon's Jeff Bezos emphasizes "disagree and commit," encouraging critical debates before uniting behind a final decision.

5. Adaptability

Dialectical leaders embrace change as an opportunity for growth, remaining flexible in the face of uncertainty.

> **Example:** Howard Schultz of Starbucks successfully adapted the company's strategy during economic downturns by refocusing on customer experience and innovation.

Strategies for Leading Dialectically

1. Create a Culture of Openness

Leaders must foster an environment where employees feel safe sharing ideas, even those that challenge conventional thinking.

> **Action Plan:**
> - Establish ground rules for respectful dialogue during meetings.
> - Actively solicit feedback from employees at all levels.

- Celebrate contributions that spark constructive debates.

  Example: Pixar's "Braintrust" meetings encourage candid feedback, allowing directors to refine their films collaboratively.

2. Embrace and Manage Conflict

Dialectical leaders view conflict as an opportunity to uncover deeper insights and drive innovation.

   Action Plan:
   - Use structured frameworks, such as role-playing or the Six Thinking Hats method, to explore conflicts from multiple angles.
   - Mediate disputes to ensure they remain constructive and focused on shared goals.

   Example: At Southwest Airlines, leadership prioritizes transparent negotiations with labor unions, turning potential conflicts into opportunities for collaboration.

3. Build Diverse Teams

Diversity in backgrounds, skills, and perspectives enhances decision-making and fosters creativity.

   Action Plan:
   - Recruit talent from underrepresented groups and diverse industries.

- Create cross-functional teams to tackle complex challenges.

- Provide training to mitigate unconscious bias in hiring and promotions.

    Example: Google's commitment to diversity has fueled breakthroughs in AI and machine learning, as varied perspectives contribute to robust solutions.

4. Balance Stability with Innovation

Leaders must preserve core values while encouraging experimentation and risk-taking.

Action Plan:

- Define and communicate non-negotiable organizational principles.

- Provide teams with the autonomy to innovate within defined boundaries.

- Establish fail-fast systems to learn quickly from unsuccessful initiatives.

    Example: Nike balances its commitment to quality and brand identity with its drive for innovation, resulting in cutting-edge products like self-lacing sneakers.

Case Studies: Dialectical Leadership in Action

Case Study 1: Satya Nadella at Microsoft

When Satya Nadella took the helm at Microsoft, the company was struggling with internal silos and declining relevance. Nadella prioritized a culture of collaboration and a growth mindset, encouraging teams to challenge traditional practices and embrace innovation.

Key Actions:

- Broke down silos by promoting cross-departmental projects.

- Shifted focus to cloud computing and AI, synthesizing Microsoft's technical strengths with emerging market opportunities.

Positive Outcome: Microsoft regained its competitive edge, becoming a leader in cloud technology and nearly tripling its market valuation.

Case Study 2: Howard Schultz at Starbucks

Howard Schultz faced a crisis during the 2008 financial downturn, as consumers cut back on discretionary spending. Schultz balanced the company's heritage of exceptional customer experiences with operational changes to adapt to the new economic reality.

Key Actions:

- Streamlined operations to reduce costs without compromising quality.

- Invested in digital innovation, including mobile ordering and loyalty programs.

Positive Outcome: Starbucks emerged stronger, maintaining its brand loyalty while achieving sustained revenue growth.

Case Study 3: Sheryl Sandberg at Facebook

As COO of Facebook, Sheryl Sandberg led the company through significant challenges, including its transition to a mobile-first platform and controversies over user privacy.

Key Actions:

- Advocated for transparency in addressing user concerns.

- Balanced the need for rapid innovation with ethical considerations.

Positive Outcome: Sandberg's leadership helped Facebook adapt to shifting consumer behaviors while reinforcing its commitment to accountability.

Developing Dialectical Leadership Skills

1. Reflect and Self-Assess

Leaders should regularly evaluate their decision-making processes, biases, and communication styles.

Action Plan: Use tools like 360-degree feedback or journaling to identify areas for improvement.

2. Practice Dialectical Thinking

Engage in exercises that challenge assumptions and encourage synthesis.

Action Plan: Use case studies or real-world scenarios to explore thesis-antithesis-synthesis dynamics.

3. Foster Continuous Learning

Leaders should stay informed about industry trends and seek opportunities to expand their knowledge.

Action Plan: Attend leadership workshops, read widely, and network with peers across industries.

Conclusion

Dialectical leaders are catalysts for transformation. By synthesizing opposing ideas, fostering collaboration, and modeling adaptability, they inspire teams to achieve extraordinary results. As organizations embrace dialectical thinking, leaders play a pivotal role in driving its integration, setting the stage for long-term success. The final chapter will explore how these principles extend beyond business, contributing to personal growth and societal progress.

Chapter 10: Beyond Business: Dialectics in Personal Growth and Society

Dialectical Thinking and Personal Development

The principles of dialectical thinking are not limited to organizations—they can also serve as powerful tools for individual growth. By applying thesis-antithesis-synthesis to personal challenges, individuals can navigate complexity, resolve internal conflicts, and continuously evolve.

Key Benefits of Dialectical Thinking in Personal Growth

1. **Self-Awareness:** Encourages reflection on one's values, beliefs, and assumptions.

2. **Resilience:** Helps individuals adapt to change and overcome obstacles.

3. **Empathy:** Fosters understanding and appreciation of diverse perspectives.

Applying Dialectical Thinking to Everyday Life

1. Resolving Internal Conflicts

We all face internal contradictions—desires that clash with responsibilities or ambitions that conflict with current realities. Dialectical thinking provides a framework for reconciling these tensions.

> **Example:** Balancing career aspirations (thesis) with personal well-being (antithesis) can lead to a synthesis, such as prioritizing jobs that align with personal values and offer flexibility.

2. Navigating Change

Change, whether personal or professional, often brings uncertainty. Dialectical thinking enables individuals to embrace the tension between holding onto familiar routines and exploring new opportunities.

> **Example:** Moving to a new city involves maintaining connections to one's roots (thesis) while building a new community (antithesis). The synthesis might be integrating old and new relationships for a richer social network.

3. Building Stronger Relationships

Effective relationships require understanding and integrating differing perspectives. Dialectical thinking encourages active listening and collaborative problem-solving.

Example: In a disagreement with a partner, acknowledging each other's needs (antithesis) can lead to solutions that strengthen the relationship.

Dialectical Thinking in Society

At a societal level, dialectical thinking has the potential to address complex challenges, bridging divides and fostering collaboration across diverse groups.

1. Social Innovation

Social progress often arises from the clash of traditional practices with emerging ideas. Dialectical thinking can help reconcile these tensions, leading to innovative solutions.

> **Example:** The global transition to renewable energy represents a synthesis of industrial growth (thesis) and environmental preservation (antithesis).

2. Bridging Polarization

In an era of increasing societal divides, dialectical thinking offers a path to mutual understanding. By acknowledging the validity of differing perspectives, societies can find common ground.

> **Example:** Dialogues on public health policies, such as vaccine distribution, benefit from synthesizing scientific expertise with community concerns to develop equitable strategies.

3. Addressing Global Challenges

Complex global issues—climate change, poverty, and inequality—demand collaborative, dialectical approaches that integrate diverse viewpoints and disciplines.

> **Example:** The Paris Agreement on climate change synthesizes the priorities of developed and developing nations to create a unified framework for reducing emissions.

Case Studies: Dialectics in Action

Case Study 1: Truth and Reconciliation in South Africa

Following the end of apartheid, South Africa faced the challenge of addressing decades of systemic injustice while fostering national unity.

Dialectical Approach:

- **Thesis:** Justice for victims.
- **Antithesis:** Forgiveness to avoid cycles of retribution.
- **Synthesis:** The Truth and Reconciliation Commission, which provided a platform for acknowledging atrocities while promoting restorative justice.

Positive Outcome: South Africa avoided large-scale violence, setting a global example for post-conflict reconciliation.

Case Study 2: The European Union

The European Union (EU) arose from the need to reconcile the sovereignty of individual nations with the benefits of regional cooperation.

Dialectical Approach:

- **Thesis:** National independence.

- **Antithesis:** Economic and political integration.

- **Synthesis:** A union that maintains member states' autonomy while fostering shared governance on trade, security, and environmental policies.

Positive Outcome: The EU has promoted peace, economic growth, and collaboration across diverse nations.

Case Study 3: Civil Rights Movement in the U.S.

The U.S. Civil Rights Movement reconciled the conflict between entrenched systemic racism (thesis) and demands for equality (antithesis) through nonviolent resistance and legislative change.

Dialectical Approach:

- **Thesis:** Preservation of existing societal structures.

- **Antithesis:** Radical calls for justice and equality.

- **Synthesis:** Civil rights legislation that redefined societal norms while maintaining institutional continuity.

Positive Outcome: Landmark achievements such as the Civil Rights Act and Voting Rights Act laid the foundation for ongoing progress toward racial equality.

Cultivating Dialectical Thinking for a Better Society

1. Promote Education and Awareness

Teaching dialectical principles in schools, workplaces, and communities fosters critical thinking and empathy.

> **Action Plan:** Incorporate thesis-antithesis-synthesis exercises into curricula and training programs.

2. Encourage Dialogue Across Divides

Structured dialogues between opposing groups can reduce polarization and build mutual understanding.

> **Action Plan:** Facilitate town halls, debate forums, and mediation programs that emphasize listening and collaboration.

3. Support Collaborative Problem-Solving

Tackle societal challenges through interdisciplinary and

cross-sector collaboration.

Action Plan: Establish partnerships between governments, businesses, and nonprofits to co-create solutions.

Vision for a Dialectical Future

Imagine a world where individuals, organizations, and societies consistently embrace dialectical thinking. This vision includes:

1. **Empowered Individuals:** People who navigate life's complexities with confidence, resilience, and empathy.

2. **Innovative Organizations:** Businesses that thrive by integrating diverse perspectives and continuously evolving.

3. **Collaborative Societies:** Communities that bridge divides and tackle global challenges through shared purpose.

Achieving the Vision

- **Practice:** Apply dialectical thinking in everyday decisions.

- **Share:** Advocate for its principles within your networks.

- **Lead:** Inspire others by embodying dialectical approaches in your personal and professional life.

Conclusion: Your Dialectical Journey Ahead

Dialectical thinking is more than a framework—it is a mindset for navigating a complex, interconnected world. Whether applied to personal growth, business challenges, or societal progress, its principles empower us to transform conflicts into opportunities, tensions into breakthroughs, and divisions into unity.

As you move forward, let this book serve as your guide and inspiration. Embrace the journey of synthesis, and use it to create a more innovative, inclusive, and resilient future—for yourself, your organization, and the world.

Chapter 11: Harnessing Technology for Dialectical Innovation

The Intersection of Technology and Dialectical Thinking

Technology has become an integral tool for modern businesses, enabling faster decision-making, deeper insights, and greater connectivity. In the context of dialectical thinking, technology serves as both a catalyst and an enabler. It provides the means to gather diverse perspectives, simulate complex scenarios, and synthesize innovative solutions.

Key Roles of Technology in Dialectical Thinking

1. **Data-Driven Insights:** Technology enables organizations to analyze vast amounts of data, uncovering patterns and contradictions that inform decision-making.

2. **Collaboration Platforms:** Digital tools foster cross-functional communication, ensuring that diverse perspectives are represented in the decision-making process.

3. **Simulation and Modeling:** Advanced technologies allow businesses to test and refine ideas in virtual environments, reducing risk and improving outcomes.

Leveraging Technology for Dialectical Processes

1. Artificial Intelligence (AI) and Machine Learning

AI and machine learning are transforming how organizations synthesize information and make decisions. These technologies can identify trends, generate predictive models, and highlight potential conflicts or opportunities.

> **Use Case:** AI-driven tools can analyze customer feedback to identify competing demands (e.g., price sensitivity vs. premium quality) and suggest optimized solutions.

2. Big Data Analytics

Big data analytics enables organizations to analyze large, complex datasets to identify contradictions and opportunities that might otherwise go unnoticed.

> **Example:** Retailers use data analytics to reconcile competing customer preferences, such as the desire for personalized experiences (thesis) with concerns about data privacy (antithesis).

3. Virtual Reality (VR) and Augmented Reality (AR)

VR and AR technologies allow teams to visualize complex problems and explore solutions in immersive environments.

- **Example:** In urban planning, VR tools enable stakeholders to experience proposed designs, balancing functional requirements with aesthetic considerations.

4. Cloud-Based Collaboration Tools

Platforms like Slack, Microsoft Teams, and Trello facilitate real-time communication and collaboration, breaking down silos and integrating diverse perspectives.

> **Example:** Global teams can use cloud-based tools to work collaboratively on projects, synthesizing inputs from different cultural and professional backgrounds.

Case Studies: Technology-Driven Dialectical Innovation

Case Study 1: Tesla's Use of AI for Autonomous Vehicles

Tesla's journey toward self-driving cars exemplifies the dialectical process of reconciling technological innovation (thesis) with safety and regulatory concerns (antithesis).

Technology's Role:

- AI algorithms process massive datasets to improve the accuracy of Tesla's Autopilot system.

- Simulation tools allow Tesla to test scenarios virtually, identifying potential risks and refining performance.

Positive Outcome: Tesla has advanced the field of autonomous driving, synthesizing cutting-edge technology with public safety priorities.

Case Study 2: Procter & Gamble's Consumer Insights

Procter & Gamble (P&G) uses big data analytics to understand conflicting customer preferences, such as the desire for environmentally friendly products (thesis) versus affordability (antithesis).

Technology's Role:

- Data platforms aggregate consumer feedback from surveys, social media, and purchase patterns.

- AI tools analyze this data to identify trends and propose sustainable yet cost-effective solutions.

Positive Outcome: P&G has successfully launched eco-friendly product lines like Tide Purclean, which balance environmental and economic considerations.

Case Study 3: Google's Cloud-Based Innovation

Google fosters a culture of innovation through its use of cloud-based tools and AI-driven platforms.

Technology's Role:

- Collaboration tools like Google Workspace enable teams across the globe to work together seamlessly.

- AI-powered analytics provide insights into user behavior, guiding the development of new products and features.

Positive Outcome: Google's ability to synthesize diverse ideas has led to groundbreaking innovations like Google Translate and Google Photos.

Steps to Integrate Technology with Dialectical Thinking

1. Invest in Data Infrastructure

Organizations must establish robust data collection, storage, and analysis systems to support informed decision-making.

> **Action Plan:** Implement data lakes and warehouses to centralize information, ensuring accessibility and usability across teams.

2. Train Employees in Digital Tools

Employees need the skills to use digital platforms effectively, enabling them to contribute to dialectical processes.

> **Action Plan:** Provide training on AI tools, data visualization software, and collaboration platforms.

3. Encourage Experimentation with Technology

Organizations should create safe spaces for employees to test and iterate using digital tools.

> **Action Plan:** Establish innovation labs or "sandbox" environments where teams can explore new technologies without fear of failure.

4. Align Technology with Organizational Goals

Technology investments should align with the organization's mission and dialectical processes.

> **Action Plan:** Conduct regular reviews to ensure that digital tools are enhancing, rather than hindering, collaboration and synthesis.

Challenges in Technology Integration

While technology can significantly enhance dialectical thinking, it also presents challenges:

1. **Data Overload:** Too much information can overwhelm teams and hinder decision-making.

2. **Bias in AI Algorithms:** Without careful oversight, AI systems can reinforce existing biases, undermining dialectical principles.

3. **Resistance to Adoption:** Employees may resist new technologies due to a lack of familiarity or perceived complexity.

Strategies to Overcome Challenges

1. **Simplify Data Access:** Use dashboards and visualization tools to present data in user-friendly formats.

2. **Audit AI Systems:** Regularly evaluate algorithms for fairness and accuracy.

3. **Foster a Learning Culture:** Encourage employees to embrace technology through ongoing training and support.

The Future of Dialectical Thinking with Technology

As technology continues to evolve, its potential to enhance dialectical thinking will expand. Emerging trends include:

- **AI-Driven Synthesis:** Advanced AI systems capable of identifying and synthesizing complex patterns in real time.

- **Global Collaboration Networks:** Blockchain-based platforms enabling secure, transparent collaboration across industries.

- **Human-Machine Collaboration:** Augmented intelligence systems that combine human creativity with machine efficiency.

Vision for the Future

Imagine a world where technology seamlessly integrates into dialectical processes, empowering individuals and organizations to navigate complexity with unprecedented clarity. By embracing these tools, businesses can unlock new levels of innovation, resilience, and growth.

Conclusion

Harnessing technology for dialectical innovation is not just a competitive advantage—it is a necessity. By integrating digital tools into their processes, organizations can amplify their ability to synthesize opposing ideas and drive transformative outcomes. The next chapter will examine real-world failures, exploring how the absence of dialectical thinking can lead to missed opportunities and setbacks.

Chapter 12: Case Studies of Failure: When Dialectical Thinking Was Missing

The Cost of Ignoring Dialectical Thinking

While dialectical thinking empowers organizations to navigate complexity and foster innovation, its absence often leads to stagnation, missed opportunities, or outright failure. When businesses fail to synthesize competing ideas or adapt to change, they risk becoming irrelevant in an increasingly dynamic market.

Common Pitfalls of Non-Dialectical Thinking

1. **Tunnel Vision:** Overcommitting to a single perspective or strategy while ignoring alternative viewpoints.

2. **Resistance to Change:** Failing to adapt to market or technological shifts due to fear or inertia.

3. **Conflict Avoidance:** Suppressing disagreements instead of using them as opportunities for growth.

Case Studies of Missed Synthesis

Case Study 1: Kodak's Resistance to Digital Photography

Kodak was a pioneer in photography, inventing the first digital camera in 1975. However, the company focused on protecting its profitable film business (thesis) while ignoring the growing digital revolution (antithesis).

What Went Wrong:

- Kodak resisted adopting digital technology out of fear it would cannibalize its film business.
- Leadership failed to synthesize digital innovation with Kodak's core strengths in imaging.

Outcome: Kodak filed for bankruptcy in 2012, overtaken by companies that embraced digital photography, such as Canon and Sony.

Key Lesson: Organizations must reconcile the tension between legacy systems and disruptive innovation to remain competitive.

Case Study 2: Blockbuster's Decline

Blockbuster dominated the video rental market in the 1990s, but the rise of online streaming services posed a significant challenge. When Netflix offered a partnership to build a digital streaming platform, Blockbuster declined.

What Went Wrong:

- Blockbuster clung to its brick-and-mortar model (thesis), dismissing the potential of online streaming (antithesis).
- Leadership underestimated the rapid shift in consumer behavior toward digital convenience.

Outcome: Netflix, once dismissed by Blockbuster, became a streaming giant, while Blockbuster filed for bankruptcy in 2010.

Key Lesson: Organizations must remain open to new business models, even when they challenge existing revenue streams.

Case Study 3: Nokia's Mobile Phone Collapse

In the early 2000s, Nokia was the global leader in mobile phones. However, the company failed to adapt to the rise of smartphones, particularly Apple's iPhone and Android devices.

What Went Wrong:

- Nokia focused on hardware innovation (thesis) while neglecting the importance of software ecosystems (antithesis).

- Internal silos and resistance to change stifled collaboration and innovation.

Outcome: Nokia's market share plummeted, and it was eventually acquired by Microsoft in 2013.

Key Lesson: Success requires integrating complementary innovations, such as hardware and software, to meet evolving customer expectations.

Case Study 4: Toys "R" Us and E-Commerce

Toys "R" Us was a beloved toy retailer but failed to adapt to the rise of e-commerce. The company outsourced its online sales to Amazon, effectively handing over its digital strategy to a competitor.

What Went Wrong:

- Leadership prioritized physical retail stores (thesis) while neglecting the growing importance of e-commerce (antithesis).
- The company failed to synthesize a cohesive omnichannel strategy.

Outcome: Toys "R" Us declared bankruptcy in 2017, unable to compete with Amazon and other e-commerce giants.

Key Lesson: Businesses must embrace and integrate digital strategies to remain relevant in an increasingly online marketplace.

The Underlying Causes of Failure

These case studies reveal common themes that contributed to organizational failure:

1. **Short-Term Focus:** Prioritizing immediate profits over long-term sustainability.

2. **Lack of Vision:** Failing to anticipate or adapt to market and technological shifts.

3. **Inflexible Culture:** Resisting new ideas or approaches due to entrenched mindsets.

How Dialectical Thinking Could Have Helped

1. Reconciling Legacy and Innovation

In each case, dialectical thinking could have helped organizations balance the strengths of their existing models with the opportunities presented by emerging trends.

> **Example:** Kodak could have leveraged its expertise in imaging to become a leader in digital photography, rather than clinging to film.

2. Encouraging Open Dialogue

By fostering a culture of collaboration and dissent, these organizations could have surfaced alternative perspectives that challenged conventional wisdom.

Example: Blockbuster might have recognized the potential of streaming if leadership had actively sought input from innovators and front-line employees.

3. Testing and Iteration

Dialectical thinking emphasizes experimentation, allowing organizations to test new approaches without fully abandoning their core business.

Example: Toys "R" Us could have piloted its own e-commerce platform alongside its physical stores, gradually transitioning to an omnichannel model.

Preventing Future Failures with Dialectical Thinking

Organizations can learn from these failures by adopting proactive strategies that integrate dialectical principles:

1. Embrace a Growth Mindset

Encourage leaders and employees to view challenges as opportunities for learning and growth.

Action Plan: Provide training on adaptability and resilience, emphasizing the value of synthesis in navigating change.

2. Build Systems for Feedback

Create structures that facilitate open dialogue and capture diverse perspectives.

Action Plan: Use tools like suggestion boxes, regular town halls, or cross-functional teams to surface and evaluate new ideas.

3. Develop Dual Strategies

Adopt a dual-strategy approach that balances existing operations with investments in innovation.

> **Action Plan:** Allocate resources to both core business areas and experimental initiatives, ensuring flexibility and adaptability.

Conclusion

The absence of dialectical thinking in the cases of Kodak, Blockbuster, Nokia, and Toys "R" Us underscores its critical role in modern business. By synthesizing opposing ideas and adapting to change, organizations can avoid the pitfalls of rigidity and thrive in an evolving landscape. The next chapter will focus on developing practical tools and exercises for strengthening dialectical thinking in individuals and teams.

Chapter 13: Dialectics and Emotional Intelligence

The Synergy Between Dialectics and Emotional Intelligence

Emotional intelligence (EI) is the ability to understand, manage, and influence emotions—both one's own and those of others. When combined with dialectical thinking, EI enhances the capacity to navigate conflicts, foster collaboration, and synthesize diverse perspectives into innovative solutions.

Why Emotional Intelligence Matters in Dialectical Thinking

1. **Facilitates Understanding:** EI helps leaders and teams empathize with opposing viewpoints, fostering mutual respect.

2. **Builds Trust:** Emotional awareness creates an environment of psychological safety, encouraging open dialogue.

3. **Manages Conflict:** EI equips individuals to handle disagreements constructively, transforming them into opportunities for growth.

By integrating EI with dialectical principles, individuals and organizations can achieve deeper connections, more effective problem-solving, and sustained success.

The Four Pillars of Emotional Intelligence in Dialectics

1. Self-Awareness

Self-awareness involves recognizing and understanding one's emotions, strengths, and limitations. It is the foundation for managing personal biases and approaching conflicts with objectivity.

> **Example in Action:** A project manager frustrated by delays acknowledges their emotional response before engaging their team, ensuring their feedback is constructive.

2. Self-Regulation

Self-regulation is the ability to control emotional impulses and respond thoughtfully. It enables individuals to remain calm and composed, even in high-pressure situations.

> **Example in Action:** During a heated debate, a leader uses deep breathing techniques to maintain composure, facilitating a productive discussion rather than escalating tension.

3. Social Awareness

Social awareness is the ability to empathize with others and understand their emotions, needs, and concerns. It fosters meaningful connections and paves the way for collaborative problem-solving.

> **Example in Action:** A marketing executive considers customer concerns about sustainability when proposing a product redesign, balancing profitability with social responsibility.

4. Relationship Management

Relationship management involves building and maintaining strong, positive connections. It includes conflict resolution, effective communication, and fostering collaboration.

> **Example in Action:** A department head mediates a dispute between two teams, helping them identify shared goals and co-create a solution that satisfies both parties.

The Role of Emotional Intelligence in Conflict Resolution

1. Empathy as a Bridge

Empathy enables individuals to step into others' shoes, fostering understanding and reducing defensiveness during conflicts.

> **Action Plan:** Use active listening techniques, such as paraphrasing and validating emotions, to demonstrate empathy in challenging conversations.

2. Managing Emotional Reactions

High-stakes conflicts often trigger emotional responses that can derail discussions. EI helps individuals recognize and manage these reactions to stay focused on solutions.

> **Action Plan:** Encourage team members to pause and reflect during tense moments, using calming techniques to reset their mindset.

3. Turning Conflict into Collaboration

With EI, conflicts become opportunities to uncover hidden insights and generate innovative solutions.

> **Action Plan:** Frame disagreements as joint problem-solving exercises, emphasizing shared goals and mutual benefits.

Case Studies: Emotional Intelligence in Dialectical Thinking

Case Study 1: Nelson Mandela's Leadership

Nelson Mandela's leadership during South Africa's transition from apartheid exemplifies the integration of EI and dialectical thinking. Mandela balanced calls for justice (thesis) with the need for national unity (antithesis).

Emotional Intelligence in Action:

- Demonstrated empathy for both oppressed and oppressors, fostering dialogue between opposing groups.

- Regulated his own emotions, prioritizing reconciliation over retaliation.

Positive Outcome: Mandela's leadership resulted in the Truth and Reconciliation Commission, which addressed systemic injustices while promoting healing and collaboration.

Case Study 2: Satya Nadella's Cultural Transformation at Microsoft

When Satya Nadella became CEO, Microsoft faced a fragmented culture resistant to change. By leveraging EI, Nadella fostered openness and collaboration, transforming the company's approach to innovation.

Emotional Intelligence in Action:

- Listened actively to employees' concerns, building trust and engagement.

- Modelled a growth mindset, encouraging teams to learn from failures and embrace challenges.

Positive Outcome: Microsoft's cultural shift enabled it to regain market relevance, achieving leadership in cloud computing and artificial intelligence.

Case Study 3: Starbucks and Employee Relations

Starbucks has faced conflicts with employees over wages and working conditions. The company's leadership leveraged EI to address these tensions constructively.

Emotional Intelligence in Action:

- Hosted open forums to listen to employees' grievances and acknowledge their emotions.

- Implemented changes to wages and benefits, demonstrating a commitment to employee well-being.

Positive Outcome: Starbucks improved employee satisfaction and strengthened its reputation as a socially responsible employer.

Practical Tools for Cultivating Emotional Intelligence in Dialectical Thinking

1. Journaling for Self-Awareness

Encourage individuals to reflect on their emotions, triggers, and thought patterns through journaling.

> **Exercise:** Write daily entries about challenges faced, emotions experienced, and lessons learned.

2. Active Listening Training

Provide workshops that teach employees how to listen empathetically and respond constructively.

Key Techniques:
- Maintain eye contact.
- Avoid interrupting.
- Summarize what the speaker has said to confirm understanding.

3. Conflict Role-Playing

Simulate real-world scenarios where participants practice navigating conflicts using EI and dialectical thinking.

> **Exercise:** Divide participants into groups and assign roles in a challenging situation. Debrief to identify effective strategies and areas for improvement.

4. Emotional Regulation Techniques

Teach strategies for managing emotions, such as mindfulness meditation, deep breathing, or visualization.

> **Exercise:** Begin meetings with a brief mindfulness session to set a calm, focused tone.

Conclusion

Emotional intelligence is a critical enabler of dialectical thinking, transforming conflicts into opportunities for growth and innovation. By cultivating self-awareness, empathy, and relationship management skills, individuals and organizations can navigate complexity with confidence and clarity. The next chapter will explore tools and exercises for building dialectical thinking skills, empowering readers to apply these principles in their personal and professional lives.

Chapter 14: Building Dialectical Thinking Skills

The Importance of Developing Dialectical Thinking

Dialectical thinking is not an innate skill—it is a mindset and practice that can be cultivated through intentional effort. By developing this ability, individuals can approach problems with greater creativity, manage conflicts constructively, and synthesize solutions that integrate diverse perspectives.

Benefits of Dialectical Thinking

1. **Enhanced Problem-Solving:** Encourages holistic analysis and innovative solutions.

2. **Improved Decision-Making:** Balances competing priorities with clarity and foresight.

3. **Stronger Relationships:** Builds understanding and alignment among diverse stakeholders.

Core Components of Dialectical Thinking

1. Embracing Complexity

Dialectical thinkers view problems as multifaceted, recognizing the value of exploring contradictions and tensions.

> **Practice:** Seek out opposing viewpoints when faced with a challenge, actively looking for nuance and complexity.

2. Balancing Opposing Ideas

Instead of choosing between competing perspectives, dialectical thinkers aim to synthesize them into a cohesive whole.

> **Practice:** Use tools like pros and cons lists or SWOT analysis to evaluate conflicting ideas and identify integrative solutions.

3. Continuous Learning

Dialectical thinking involves adapting to new information and refining one's understanding over time.

Practice: Regularly review past decisions to identify lessons learned and areas for improvement.

Exercises for Developing Dialectical Thinking

1. Thesis-Antithesis-Synthesis Brainstorm

This exercise helps individuals and teams practice synthesizing opposing ideas into innovative solutions.

Steps:

- Define the thesis (current perspective or approach).

- Identify the antithesis (conflicting perspective or challenge).

- Brainstorm possible syntheses that integrate elements of both.

Example: In a product development meeting, balance the need for cost efficiency (thesis) with customer demands for premium features (antithesis) by brainstorming value-engineering solutions (synthesis).

2. Devil's Advocate Sessions

Encourage teams to explore alternative viewpoints by assigning someone to play the role of devil's advocate.

Steps:

1. Present a proposed idea or decision.

2. Assign a team member to challenge the idea, highlighting potential flaws or risks.

3. Use the critique to refine and strengthen the proposal.

   Benefits: Builds resilience against groupthink and surfaces hidden risks or opportunities.

3. Reflective Journaling

Journaling helps individuals process their thoughts, identify biases, and explore alternative perspectives.

Prompts:

- "What assumptions am I making about this situation?"

- "How might someone with an opposing view approach this problem?"

- "What would a synthesis of these perspectives look like?"

4. Scenario Analysis

Scenario analysis helps teams evaluate multiple potential outcomes and develop flexible strategies.

Steps:

1. Identify key variables influencing the decision (e.g., market trends, customer behaviors).
2. Develop plausible scenarios based on these variables.
3. Brainstorm strategies that address the challenges and opportunities in each scenario.

Example: A retail company might analyze scenarios involving economic growth, stagnation, or recession to create adaptive strategies.

5. Role Reversal

Role-playing encourages empathy by having participants take on perspectives different from their own.

Steps:

1. Divide participants into groups representing different stakeholders in a conflict or decision.

2. Have each group articulate the perspective, priorities, and concerns of their assigned role.

3. Facilitate a discussion to identify common ground and potential syntheses.

Example: In a corporate restructuring, one group might represent employees, another management, and a third shareholders, working together to find balanced solutions.

Tools for Supporting Dialectical Thinking

1. Mind Mapping

Mind maps visually organize complex problems, showing relationships between ideas and facilitating synthesis.

> **Use Case:** During strategic planning, use a mind map to connect organizational goals, challenges, and opportunities.

2. Collaborative Platforms

Tools like Miro, Trello, and Microsoft Teams support real-time collaboration, enabling teams to share and integrate diverse perspectives.

> **Use Case:** Use collaborative platforms to document and refine ideas during brainstorming sessions.

3. Decision Matrices

Decision matrices help teams evaluate multiple options based on predefined criteria, ensuring a balanced approach.

> **Use Case:** In selecting a new supplier, evaluate options based on cost, quality, and reliability.

Case Studies: Dialectical Thinking in Practice

Case Study 1: Amazon's Expansion Strategy

Amazon balances its focus on core retail operations (thesis) with bold investments in new ventures like AWS and Alexa (antithesis).

Dialectical Approach:

- Conducts iterative testing and refinement to integrate innovation with operational excellence.

- Uses customer feedback loops to align new initiatives with core business values.

Positive Outcome: Amazon has become a leader in multiple industries by synthesizing stability with innovation.

Case Study 2: IBM's Pivot to AI

IBM transitioned from traditional hardware to AI and cloud computing, balancing its legacy strengths (thesis) with the need to innovate (antithesis).

Dialectical Approach:

- Engaged cross-functional teams to co-create solutions.

- Used design thinking workshops to align new products with customer needs.

Positive Outcome: IBM repositioned itself as a leader in enterprise AI, revitalizing its relevance in the tech industry.

Tips for Sustained Practice

1. Start Small

Begin by applying dialectical thinking to smaller decisions before scaling to complex challenges.

2. Practice Regularly

Incorporate exercises like journaling or scenario analysis into daily routines to reinforce skills.

3. Encourage Team Participation

Foster a culture where teams regularly engage in dialectical practices, such as brainstorming and devil's advocate sessions.

4. Measure Progress

Use metrics like decision quality, team alignment, and innovation outcomes to evaluate the impact of dialectical thinking.

Conclusion

Building dialectical thinking skills empowers individuals and teams to navigate complexity with creativity, resilience, and clarity. By practicing techniques like thesis-antithesis-synthesis brainstorming, role reversal, and scenario analysis, organizations can embed this powerful approach into their culture. The next chapter will delve into how dialectical thinking can be integrated into leadership development programs to prepare the next generation of leaders for the challenges of the modern world.

Chapter 15: Dialectical Thinking in Leadership Development Programs

The Need for Dialectical Thinking in Leadership

Leadership in today's complex world requires more than technical expertise or traditional management skills. Leaders must navigate competing priorities, resolve conflicts, and synthesize diverse perspectives—all while fostering innovation and adaptability. Dialectical thinking offers a critical framework for addressing these challenges, making it a vital component of leadership development programs.

Why Dialectical Thinking is Essential for Leaders

1. **Strategic Agility:** Leaders must balance short-term objectives with long-term goals.

2. **Conflict Resolution:** Effective leadership requires managing and synthesizing opposing views.

3. **Decision-Making Excellence:** Dialectical thinking enables leaders to make well-rounded, innovative decisions in uncertain environments.

Designing Leadership Programs Around Dialectical Thinking

1. Establish Core Competencies

Leadership development programs should define the specific competencies that dialectical thinking enhances, including:

- Critical thinking and analysis.
- Emotional intelligence and empathy.
- Conflict resolution and collaboration.
- Visionary and adaptive leadership.

2. Integrate Dialectical Principles

Programs should weave dialectical thinking into every aspect of the curriculum, from strategic planning to team management.

Key Components:

- Teaching the thesis-antithesis-synthesis framework.

- Emphasizing the role of constructive conflict in driving innovation.

- Highlighting the importance of continuous learning and adaptability.

Components of a Dialectical Leadership Curriculum

1. Workshops on Complex Problem-Solving

Interactive workshops teach leaders to analyze multifaceted problems and identify syntheses that balance competing demands.

Structure:

- Present a real-world case study with conflicting priorities.

- Divide participants into groups to explore different perspectives.

- Facilitate a synthesis discussion to generate integrative solutions.

Example Case: A healthcare organization deciding between cost-cutting measures (thesis) and maintaining high patient care standards (antithesis).

2. Role-Playing and Simulations

Simulations immerse leaders in challenging scenarios, allowing them to practice navigating conflicts and synthesizing opposing ideas.

Example Exercise:

- Assign participants roles in a corporate restructuring scenario, such as executives, employees, and shareholders.

- Encourage teams to articulate their perspectives and collaboratively develop a strategy that addresses all stakeholders' concerns.

3. Emotional Intelligence Training

Emotional intelligence (EI) is essential for understanding and synthesizing diverse viewpoints. Training should focus on:

- Self-awareness and self-regulation.

- Empathy and social awareness.

- Relationship management and conflict resolution.

    Example Activity: Use empathy mapping exercises to help leaders understand stakeholder emotions and priorities during conflicts.

4. Cross-Functional Collaboration Projects

Encourage participants to work on projects that require input from multiple departments or disciplines.

- **Objective:** Teach leaders to navigate complexity by integrating diverse expertise and priorities.

- **Example Project:** Develop a strategy for launching a new product that aligns marketing, R&D, and operations teams.

5. Reflective Practices

Reflection helps leaders internalize dialectical principles and identify areas for growth.

Activities:

- Daily journaling prompts, such as: "What opposing viewpoints did I encounter today, and how did I address them?"

- Group debriefs after simulations to discuss lessons learned and strategies for improvement.

Case Studies: Dialectical Thinking in Leadership Development

Case Study 1: GE's Crotonville Leadership Academy

General Electric (GE) incorporates dialectical thinking into its Crotonville leadership development programs. Leaders are exposed to scenarios requiring them to balance innovation with operational efficiency.

Key Features:

- Role-playing exercises to navigate conflicts between short-term shareholder expectations and long-term R&D investments.

- Workshops on thesis-antithesis-synthesis to craft balanced strategies.

Positive Outcome: GE's leadership alumni are known for their ability to manage complexity and drive organizational success.

Case Study 2: McKinsey & Company's Leadership Training

McKinsey's leadership programs emphasize collaboration, adaptability, and decision-making under uncertainty. Dialectical principles are embedded in exercises like conflict resolution simulations and stakeholder analysis.

Key Features:

- Teams work on high-stakes, real-world business cases.
- Leaders are challenged to synthesize opposing priorities, such as cost reduction and customer experience.

Positive Outcome: McKinsey's approach equips leaders to thrive in ambiguous, high-pressure environments.

Case Study 3: Google's Leadership Development

Google's "g2g" (Googler-to-Googler) training program integrates dialectical thinking by encouraging employees to question assumptions and explore diverse perspectives.

Key Features:

- Peer-led workshops on critical thinking and emotional intelligence.

- Tools for collaborative problem-solving in cross-functional teams.

Positive Outcome: Google's culture of openness and synthesis drives its continued innovation and global influence.

Metrics for Evaluating Success

1. Decision-Making Quality

Track improvements in leaders' ability to make balanced, innovative decisions.

> **Metric:** Pre- and post-program evaluations of decision-making scenarios.

2. Conflict Resolution Effectiveness

Assess how well leaders resolve conflicts and foster collaboration.

> **Metric:** Feedback from team members on leaders' conflict management skills.

3. Organizational Impact

Measure the tangible outcomes of leaders' decisions, such

as project success rates and business growth.

> **Metric:** Key performance indicators (KPIs) linked to program goals.

Overcoming Challenges in Leadership Development

Challenge 1: Resistance to New Approaches

Some leaders may be skeptical of dialectical methods, preferring traditional decision-making models.

> **Solution:** Highlight the real-world benefits of dialectical thinking through case studies and success stories.

Challenge 2: Limited Time for Training

Busy leaders may struggle to dedicate time to development programs.

> **Solution:** Offer flexible formats, such as online modules and on-the-job applications.

Challenge 3: Cultural Barriers

Organizations with rigid hierarchies may resist collaborative approaches.

Solution: Start with pilot programs to demonstrate the value of dialectical leadership.

Conclusion

Integrating dialectical thinking into leadership development programs prepares leaders to navigate complexity, resolve conflicts, and drive innovation. By incorporating workshops, simulations, and cross-functional projects, organizations can equip their leaders with the tools they need to thrive in a dynamic world. The next chapter will explore cultural influences on dialectical thinking, examining how global perspectives shape its application and effectiveness.

Chapter 16: Cultural Impacts on Dialectical Thinking

The Influence of Culture on Dialectical Thinking

Culture plays a significant role in shaping how individuals and organizations approach problem-solving, decision-making, and conflict resolution. Dialectical thinking, with its emphasis on synthesis and integration, is deeply influenced by cultural norms, values, and worldviews.

Key Questions Addressed

1. How do cultural differences shape perceptions of conflict and synthesis?

2. Which cultural traits align naturally with dialectical thinking?

3. How can organizations foster dialectical thinking in multicultural environments?

Understanding these dynamics is essential for applying dialectical thinking effectively in global contexts.

Cultural Frameworks and Dialectical Thinking

1. Individualism vs. Collectivism

Cultures vary in their emphasis on individual goals (individualism) versus group harmony (collectivism).

Individualist Cultures:

- Prioritize personal autonomy and self-expression.

- Tend to view conflict as a natural part of individual rights.

    Example: The United States often embraces debate and diverse viewpoints, fostering innovation but sometimes struggling with synthesis.

    Collectivist Cultures:

- Emphasize group cohesion and consensus.

- Prefer conflict avoidance but excel at finding harmonious solutions.

    Example: Japan's approach to decision-making (nemawashi) involves extensive pre-meeting discussions to build consensus before formal decisions.

2. High-Context vs. Low-Context Communication

Communication styles influence how conflicts and contradictions are expressed and resolved.

High-Context Cultures:

- Rely on implicit communication, with meaning derived from context and relationships.
- May avoid direct confrontation but excel at nuanced synthesis.

    Example: Chinese business culture often prioritizes maintaining face and resolving tensions indirectly through mediation.

Low-Context Cultures:

- Favor explicit, direct communication, with a focus on clarity.
- Engage openly in debate, though this can sometimes escalate conflicts.

    Example: German business culture values precision and directness, often leading to well-defined but uncompromising solutions.

3. Power Distance

Power distance refers to the extent to which a culture accepts hierarchical authority.

High Power Distance Cultures:

- Respect for hierarchy may limit open expression of opposing views.

- Leaders play a critical role in facilitating synthesis.

    Example: In India, deference to seniority often means that leaders must actively encourage participation to surface diverse perspectives.

Low Power Distance Cultures:

- Encourage egalitarian relationships, fostering open dialogue.

- May struggle with decisiveness if consensus-building stalls.

    Example: Scandinavian countries' flat organizational structures facilitate collaborative synthesis but require strong facilitation to drive decisions.

Case Studies: Cultural Variations in Dialectical Thinking

Case Study 1: Chinese Yin-Yang Philosophy

Chinese culture's deep-rooted yin-yang philosophy aligns naturally with dialectical thinking. It emphasizes the interdependence of opposites and the dynamic balance between them.

Application:

- Businesses in China often integrate competing priorities, such as innovation (yang) and tradition (yin), to craft holistic strategies.

Positive Outcome: Alibaba's dual strategy of blending cutting-edge e-commerce with traditional retail exemplifies yin-yang synthesis in action.

Case Study 2: American Entrepreneurial Spirit

The United States' individualistic culture fosters dialectical thinking through open debate and risk-taking. However, its emphasis on competition can sometimes hinder synthesis.

Application:

- Silicon Valley's innovation culture thrives on challenging norms and integrating diverse perspectives, though it occasionally struggles with internal alignment.

Positive Outcome: Companies like Apple synthesize user-centric design with technological innovation, achieving global success.

Case Study 3: Scandinavian Consensus-Building

Scandinavian countries prioritize collaboration and equality, aligning well with dialectical principles.

Application:

- Organizations like IKEA emphasize co-creation and cross-functional collaboration, integrating diverse inputs into unified strategies.

Positive Outcome: IKEA's flat hierarchy and inclusive culture have enabled it to adapt to global markets while staying true to its Swedish roots.

Strategies for Fostering Dialectical Thinking Across Cultures

1. Understand Cultural Strengths

Identify how cultural traits align with dialectical thinking and leverage these strengths.

Action Plan:
- Conduct cultural awareness training for teams working in global contexts.
- Highlight examples of successful synthesis within each culture.

2. Encourage Cross-Cultural Collaboration

Create opportunities for teams from different cultural backgrounds to work together, fostering mutual understanding and shared learning.

Action Plan:

- Use structured frameworks, such as role-playing exercises, to surface and integrate diverse perspectives.

- Pair teams from high-context and low-context cultures to balance implicit and explicit communication styles.

3. Adapt Facilitation Techniques

Tailor conflict resolution and decision-making processes to cultural preferences.

Action Plan:

- In collectivist cultures, use pre-meeting discussions to build consensus.

- In individualist cultures, encourage open debate but set clear ground rules to guide synthesis.

4. Develop Globally Minded Leaders

Train leaders to navigate cultural differences and foster dialectical thinking in multicultural teams.

Action Plan:

- Incorporate intercultural communication and emotional intelligence training into leadership development programs.

- Use real-world case studies to demonstrate how successful leaders synthesize global perspectives.

Overcoming Cultural Barriers

1. Addressing Resistance to Synthesis

Some cultures may resist synthesis due to a preference for clear winners and losers.

> **Solution:** Frame synthesis as a win-win outcome that enhances collective success.

2. Navigating Language Barriers

Miscommunication can hinder the expression of opposing ideas in multicultural teams.

> **Solution:** Use visual tools like mind maps or diagrams to bridge language gaps.

3. Managing Time Zone Differences

Global teams may face logistical challenges in collaborating effectively.

> **Solution:** Implement asynchronous communication tools and schedule meetings strategically to maximize participation.

Conclusion

Culture shapes how dialectical thinking is expressed, embraced, and applied. By understanding and leveraging cultural differences, organizations can harness the full potential of dialectical thinking on a global scale. Whether reconciling yin-yang dynamics in Asia, fostering open debate in the West, or prioritizing consensus in Scandinavia, the principles of synthesis can bridge divides and drive innovation.

The final chapter will reflect on the journey of dialectical thinking, summarizing key insights and providing a vision for its future impact on individuals, organizations, and society.

Chapter 17: Reflections and the Future of Dialectical Thinking

The Journey of Dialectical Thinking

Over the course of this book, we have explored how dialectical thinking transforms individuals, organizations, and societies. From resolving conflicts and fostering collaboration to driving innovation and adapting to change, dialectical thinking provides a powerful framework for navigating complexity.

Key Takeaways

- **Dialectics is Universal:** Its principles apply across personal, professional, and societal contexts, offering a timeless method for integrating opposites.

- **Conflict as Opportunity:** Dialectical thinking reframes conflict as a catalyst for growth and innovation.

- **Synthesis as Progress:** By balancing competing priorities, dialectical thinking enables continuous learning and adaptation.

Dialectical Thinking in Action: A Summary

For Individuals

- **Self-Awareness:** Dialectical thinking encourages reflection on personal values and assumptions, fostering growth and resilience.

- **Decision-Making:** It provides tools for navigating ambiguity and synthesizing complex choices.

- **Relationships:** By integrating empathy with collaboration, it strengthens connections and resolves conflicts.

For Organizations

- **Innovation:** Dialectical thinking fuels creativity by reconciling diverse perspectives and challenges.

- **Leadership:** Leaders who embody dialectical principles inspire trust, adaptability, and vision.

- **Culture:** Organizations that embrace dialectical thinking thrive in dynamic environments, balancing stability with transformation.

For Society

- **Bridging Divides:** Dialectical thinking fosters dialogue and unity in polarized communities.

- **Global Collaboration:** It provides a framework for addressing shared challenges, from climate change to technological ethics.

- **Continuous Evolution:** Societies that integrate opposing ideas remain agile and resilient, paving the way for progress.

The Future of Dialectical Thinking

As the world becomes increasingly interconnected and complex, the need for dialectical thinking will only grow. Below are emerging trends and opportunities for its application in the future:

1. Technology-Driven Dialectics

The rise of artificial intelligence, big data, and digital platforms will enhance dialectical thinking by:

- **Facilitating Analysis:** AI systems can identify and synthesize diverse perspectives at scale.

- **Supporting Collaboration:** Digital tools enable global teams to work together seamlessly, integrating cultural and disciplinary differences.

2. Dialectical Leadership in a Post-Pandemic World

The COVID-19 pandemic underscored the importance of balancing health, economic, and social priorities. Future leaders will need to:

- **Navigate Uncertainty:** Synthesize short-term crisis management with long-term resilience.
- **Promote Equity:** Balance the needs of diverse stakeholders to create inclusive solutions.

3. Addressing Global Challenges

Dialectical thinking will play a critical role in solving complex, systemic issues:

- **Climate Change:** Reconciling economic development with environmental preservation.
- **Technological Ethics:** Balancing innovation with privacy, security, and equity.
- **Social Justice:** Integrating diverse perspectives to build equitable, sustainable communities.

Building a Dialectical Future

1. Education and Training

Embedding dialectical thinking into educational systems and professional training programs will empower the next generation of leaders to:

- Embrace complexity.
- Resolve conflicts constructively.
- Drive innovation in dynamic environments.

2. Cross-Sector Collaboration

Partnerships between governments, businesses, and nonprofits will leverage dialectical principles to:

- Align public and private interests.
- Foster global cooperation on shared challenges.
- Create solutions that balance efficiency with equity.

3. Personal Commitment

Individuals can contribute to a dialectical future by:

- Practicing reflection and empathy in daily life.
- Engaging in dialogue with those who hold differing viewpoints.

- Advocating for synthesis-driven solutions in their communities.

A Vision for the Future

Imagine a world where:

- Conflicts are viewed as opportunities for collaboration rather than division.
- Organizations consistently innovate by synthesizing tradition with transformation.
- Societies thrive by embracing diversity and integrating global perspectives.

This vision is not utopian; it is achievable through the consistent application of dialectical thinking. By equipping individuals, organizations, and societies with the tools to navigate complexity, we can build a future that is innovative, inclusive, and resilient.

Your Role in the Dialectical Journey

As a reader of this book, you are now part of the dialectical movement. Whether you are a leader, a collaborator, or a lifelong learner, your ability to synthesize opposing ideas will shape your impact on the world.

Next Steps:

1. **Apply the Tools:** Use the exercises and frameworks in this book to practice dialectical thinking in your daily life.

2. **Share the Vision:** Advocate for dialectical principles in your organizations and communities.

3. **Continue Learning:** Stay curious, open-minded, and committed to growth.

Together, we can create a world where complexity is embraced, conflicts are transformed, and progress is achieved through synthesis.

Conclusion

Dialectical thinking is more than a framework—it is a mindset for navigating a complex and interconnected world. Its principles empower us to transform challenges into opportunities, tensions into breakthroughs, and divisions into unity. As you move forward, let this book inspire you to embrace synthesis in every aspect of your life, creating a brighter future for yourself, your organization, and society as a whole.

www.ingramcontent.com/pod-product-compliance
Lightning Source LLC
Chambersburg PA
CBHW071546220526
45469CB00003B/936